T0285768

*Class*

THE ITALIAN LIST

# Class

ANDREA CAVALLETTI

*Translated by*
ELISA FIACCADORI

*Edited and with an Afterword by*
ALBERTO TOSCANO

LONDON  NEW YORK  CALCUTTA

SERIES EDITOR
**Alberto Toscano**

**Seagull Books, 2019**

Originally published as Andrea Cavalletti, *Classe*
© Bollati Boringhieri editore, Turin, 2009

First published in English translation by Seagull Books, 2019

English translation © Elisa Fiaccadori, 2019

Afterword © Alberto Toscano, 2019

ISBN   978 0 8574 2 437 2

**British Library Cataloguing-in-Publication Data**
A catalogue record for this book is available from the British Library

Typeset by Seagull Books, Calcutta, India
Printed and bound by Hyam Enterprises, Calcutta, India

# Contents

New Orleans is under water and the National Guard marches against the enraged crowds. The *banlieues* erupt, as does Exarchia, and the rebelling bands seem uncannily resuscitated from the dusty pages of *The Psychology of Crowds*. Indeed, Gustave Le Bon, that good old reactionary, had once let slip an explanation: 'These noisy and maleficent crowds, the kernel of all insurrections, from antiquity to our own times, are the only crowds known to the rhetorician.'[1]

To circumscribe the site that produces danger is an anti-rhetorical strategy: it also helps reveal the possibility of a rupture at the centre of the social *dispositif*.[2] Such a possibility is equivalent to the destruction of the basic and necessary conditions of the *dispositif*. And *this* destruction will not be the work of any noisy crowd . . .

---

1 Gustave Le Bon, *The Psychology of Revolution* (Bernard Miall trans.) (London: T. Fisher Unwin, 1913), p. 71.

2 [Apparatus or device—as is now common usage in the humanities, the term is left in the original French to signal its origins in the work of Michel Foucault. (This and subsequent notes in brackets are from the editor and/or the translator.)]

1. What is modern society? In his apodictic style, Jean-Claude Milner has provided a clear answer: '[I]t's the society born from the rupture of 1789–1815. Evidently, it was not established immediately, or everywhere, but an ideal was constructed.'[3] As 'the most enlightened observers of the Congress of Vienna' must have noticed, for the first time, a new type of society, and not of government, was being introduced to Europe—regardless of whether this was the seventeenth-century absolute monarchy or, in the Age of Revolution, Saint-Just's concept of republican institutions. If the political ideal had always been that of government, 'the nineteenth century, on the contrary, put society at the centre of the *dispositif*.'[4]

Now, this new organization of powers was also made possible because their new centre—a centre that combines implementation and projection—has attained a special degree of evidence: 'The emergence of society, and no longer of good government, as organizing point for a political vision of the world—this constitutes Balzac's great discovery. He made it in Paris. He couldn't have made it anywhere else. It is in Paris that we witness the clearest example of a society which, in order to remain selfsame, spends its time looking for a government, and rejects it only when its degree of adequacy falls below the tolerable.'[5]

But, Milner adds:

3 Jean-Claude Milner, *Les Penchants criminels de l'Europe démocratique* (Lagrasse: Verdier, 2003), p. 20.

4 Ibid., pp. 20–1.

5 Ibid., p. 21.

> [W]e need to generalize: the same society
> unfolds progressively on the two sides of the
> English Channel and the two sides of the North
> Atlantic, with their different types of govern-
> ments. [ . . . ] Eventually, the doctrinarians must
> constitute a model [ . . . ] to serve as the common
> denominator for all these different governments
> and to unite within itself the minimal common
> properties needed optimally to serve the ideal
> society [ . . . ] the common denominator is called
> *democracy*.[6]

Since the type of government is not the central problem, it is obvious that the advent of a regime that is no
longer democratic will not invalidate society; it is also
implicit that democracy itself can take different shapes:
plastic and ready to be transformed, it can fade off when
the degree of adequacy demands it, making way for its
apparent opposite. Carl Schmitt's position, coherent in
its own way, remains exemplary in this regard. In the
Weimar period, he saw the foundations of democracy in
acclamation and in the identity of the governing and the
governed. After 1933, he affirmed the same principles in
national-socialist terms.

Paris is not the capital of democracy but, above all,
the capital of society. Modern society, which spans all
governments and can group them all under the denom-
inator of democracy, is in the first place *unlimited*. It is
not infinite. But whatever the numbers of its members—
many or few—and no matter how broad its unfolding,
the essential thing is that it is without limits.

'Not only,' Milner writes, 'is there no existent that can
or must constitute a limit or an exception, but henceforth

6 Ibid., pp. 21–2.

the society-function includes among its possible variables any existent whatsoever, human or nonhuman, animate or inanimate. There exists nothing and no one for whom the function ceases to produce meaning. There exists nothing and no one that can suspend society.'[7]

The city is not an infinite space but the proper and unlimited domain of the social. It seems impossible, no matter where one is, to get away from Paris.

2. In 1786, Giuseppe Palmieri published his *Riflessioni sulla pubblica felicità relativamente al Regno di Napoli* (Reflections on Public Happiness Relative to the Kingdom of Naples).[8] The qualifier 'relative to' is paradigmatic. In the eighteenth century, the arts of government— German or Austrian cameralism in all its variants, the French *science de la police*, the civil economy in Italy—all still aimed at the particular; sciences changed with governments, and the migration of authors from one dominion to another, from one court to another, was followed by new editions of their treatises. Regimes could still dictate the principles of political knowledge. But, at the same time, the unique rationality of population—the true wealth of all states and the central concept for all arts of government—came to the fore. The population, to which sovereigns now had to devote their most attentive care, was not only made up of the sum total of the inhabitants of Holland or France, it was—according to the expression made famous by Étienne Noël Damilaville— the relationship between this number and the national territory. So, the number changed, as did the extension

---

7 Ibid., p. 23.

8 Giuseppe Palmieri, *Riflessioni sulla pubblica felicità relativamente al Regno di Napoli* (Napoli: Raimondi, 1787).

and characteristics of territories; but the form remained the same. Even the particular reasons of climate and *milieu* did not contradict but reaffirmed, as its variables, the general and essential function of the population. The city was in the first place a specific relationship between its inhabitants and the space they occupied; it corresponded to certain living conditions that had to be optimal. Only when this relationship no longer needed to be defined, because it had become both implicit and evident, did population make way for society. The seventeenth-century treaties stated the rules for the proper construction of the city as rules for the healthy constitution and well-being of a political body that was still novel to them. If 'the bourgeoisie has subjected the country to the rule of the towns',[9] it is because the latter has become an incontrovertible principle: the conservation of the countryside or even the ruralization of the city have become urban questions. From the nineteenth century onwards, urban planning turns out to be the discipline that is always already immersed in the social, while the social is inexorably referred back to this new discipline, which now gathers together and transforms all types of knowledge about the population.

**3.** Sociology, [Émile] Durkheim affirms, deals with facts. But it is only in the historical fold from which sociology can liberate itself but which remains obscure to it, only in the blind spot of the sociological gaze, that 'facts' acquire their character and peculiar consistency. Their patency betrays an opacity and also shows a precise constitutive mark: if social phenomena are 'concrete facts'

9 Karl Marx and Friedrich Engels, *Manifesto of the Communist Party* in *Collected Works*, VOL. 6 (London: Lawrence & Wishart, 1976), p. 488.

and are not in the least abstract; if sociology is not to devolve into mere erudition; if the true sociologist in the end always turns to facts, it is precisely because *there is nothing in the unlimited prospect of society that can stop being a fact*. It is belonging to this unlimited that produces the fact as such. And sociology maintains itself in a permanent relation with the detail of facts because, like democracy, it is a necessary expression of the social *dispositif*, which differentiates itself into various sciences and always strives towards self-regulation. In Durkheim's perspective, this indissoluble relationship that defines the true sociological task sketches itself out as a line or better as an 'evolution' of sociological facts. Inertia is not part of their nature. They are strange, mobile and changing facts. They change over time, mix and blend together because they belong to opposite categories: the healthy and the unhealthy, the normal and the pathological. Normal facts and pathological facts must be observed and collected together but they never stop generating variants that must be kept apart in order for them to be recomposed in a linear continuum that goes from the normal to the pathological and from the pathological to the normal. Durkheim's method, which recognizes qualitatively different types of society and leaves to [Auguste] Comte the idea of progress, introducing discontinuity into history instead, represents the most radical technique of integration into the timeline of evolution, that is, of the 'inclusion' of facts as such, or the unlimited constitution of the social. That each society is singularly distinguishable means that each society is 'normal' *in its* own *way*. Singularly, everything tends towards normality; there is nothing that is not social.

4. If there is a fact whose pathological character appears incontrovertible, it is crime. Durkheim, however, asks us

to consider the problem less hastily. There is no society exempt from crime, and crime will not disappear with the evolving of social conditions; it will only change form. 'Thus, since there cannot be a society in which individuals do not diverge to some extent from the collective type, it is also inevitable that among these deviations some assume a criminal character.'[10] Between the constitution of collective normality and individual originality, there is a continuous relation: *l'une ne va pas sans l'autre*, one defines the other, and, in order for society to be able to continue evolving, that which differs from the general norm must continuously come to light. As we read in *The Rules of Sociological Method* (1895):

> [C]rime itself may play a useful part in [social] evolution. Not only does it imply that the way to necessary changes remains open, but in certain cases it also directly prepares for these changes. Where crime exists, collective sentiments are not only in the state of plasticity necessary to assume a new form, but sometimes it even contributes to determining beforehand the shape they will take on.[11]

In *The Division of Labour in Society* (1893), Durkheim had unequivocally excluded the criminal from the dynamics of society. But presented with the reasons of the unlimited, sociology itself required a further adjustment. From the more correct point of view of the *Rules*, the criminal presents himself under an entirely new light as the regulator of society—and he dictates a precise political task: 'The duty of the statesman is no longer to

---

10 Émile Durkheim, *The Rules of Sociological Method* (Steven Lukes ed., W. D. Halls trans.) (New York: The Free Press, 1982), p. 101.

11 Ibid., p. 102.

propel societies violently towards an ideal which appears attractive to him. His role is rather that of the doctor: he forestalls the outbreak of sickness by maintaining good hygiene, or when it does break out, seeks to cure it.'[12] The sociologist and the statesman are akin, and their shared features are embodied in the doctor. Social sciences ascertain the tolerability of governments and warn about the emergence of excessively rigid ideals. But they must also keep pace with society, revisiting their positions and exercising caution about overly hasty exclusions. The statesman and the sociologist cannot do without the criminal, who cannot escape his 'necessary and useful' normalizing role as *agent régulier de la vie sociale,* the regulating agent of social life.[13] If social normalization is unlimited, then so is criminalization. In a double sense: not only will those sociological facts par excellence that are crime and the criminal never stop existing but, one must add, no model of normalization or integration of the phenomenon and no degree of reaction or repression can be ruled out in principle. In Durkheim, we thus

---

12 Ibid., p. 104.

13 Durkheim's text is very reminiscent of Marx's brief '[Digression (On Productive Labour)]' in the fourth volume of *Capital,* otherwise known as *Theories of Surplus Value*: 'A philosopher produces ideas, a poet poems, a clergyman sermons, a professor books and so on. A criminal produces crime. . . . Thus the criminal comes in as one of those natural "counterweights" [*natürliche "Ausgleichungen"*] which bring about a correct balance and open up a whole perspective of "useful" occupations' (Karl Marx, 'Economic Manuscript of 1861–63' in Karl Marx and Friedrich Engels, *Collected Works, Volume 30: Marx, 1861–1863* [Ben Fowkes and Emile Burns trans] [London: Lawrence & Wishart, 1988], pp. 306–9). Marx's drafts were published posthumously by Karl Kautsky in 1905, ten years after *The Rules of Sociological Method.* Thus, *agent régulier* is translated by *Ausgleichung,* and the parody precedes the original.

witness the emergence of absolute abnormality: 'It can certainly happen that crime itself has abnormal forms; this is what happens, for instance, when it reaches an excessively high level.'[14] Criminals can become 'harmful' but without thereby becoming socially irrelevant, without ever ceasing to produce meaning for democratic society, which is in turn always malleable enough to liquidate them. Even the elimination of the undesirables is a social fact.

To use Durkheim's term, in Paris nothing and nobody is *unsociable*. Paris is the place of the normalization of crime itself, whose forms, together with those of government, have to be rendered tolerable. There is an echo here of the truth about free competition, unwittingly voiced by Proudhon: '[I]t is necessary to find its equilibrium, I would be ready to say its *police*.'[15] This is not solely a matter of work or profit, and it finds its a priori in the social.

5. As Furio Jesi writes in *Spartakus*:

> You can love a city, you can recognize its houses and its streets in your remotest or dearest memories; but [ . . . o]ne appropriates a city by fleeing or advancing, charging and being charged, much more than by playing as a child in its streets or

---

14 Durkheim, *The Rules of Sociological Method*, p. 98, translation modified (the English translation has 'normal', where it should read 'abnormal').

15 Pierre-Joseph Proudhon, *Système des contradictions économiques, ou, Philosophie de la misère, Tome I* (Paris: Garnier 1850), p. 223. Quoted in Karl Marx, *The Poverty of Philosophy: Answer to the 'Philosophy of Poverty' by M. Proudhon* in Karl Marx and Friedrich Engels, *Collected Works, Volume 6: Marx and Engels, 1845–1848* (London: Lawrence & Wishart, 1976), p. 191.

strolling through it with a girl. In the hour of revolt, one is no longer alone in the city.[16]

What is a revolt? It is, Jesi explains, a suspension of the normal time established by power. But its character of pure suspension does not in any way disprove society. Rather, it condemns revolt to failure. It is precisely as the suspension of time that revolt will come to an end; and in the domain of the unlimited, the initiative will soon return to those who ordered the charges. As the *Mémoires de Monsieur Claude, Chef de la Police de sûreté sous le Second Empire* (Memoirs of M. Claude, Chief of the Security Police under the Second Empire, 1882) tell us:

> [A]fter the capitulation of the Commune, the *sûreté* service was worn out. The upheaval of the social order was less the result of our palaces' ruins and the burnt-out houses than of the confusion brought about in all administrative bodies. With regard to justice, the setting on fire of its Palace caused the destruction of the archives and of civil status records—this benefited all the criminals. As a consequence of the fact that there were no longer any criminal records, society's insurgents could define themselves as angels; fire had purified them. Perhaps on purpose? In any case, by satisfying their desires, the Commune assured their impunity. They took advantage of this, as they had taken advantage of war to seize Paris and establish their power after the retreat of the enemy. As for past epochs of war and anarchy, mobs and assassins who were to be brought to justice reappeared in the

16 Furio Jesi, *Spartakus: The Symbology of Revolt* (Andrea Cavalletti ed., Alberto Toscano trans.) (London: Seagull, 2014), pp. 54–5.

districts of the Seine, Seine-et-Marne and Seine-et-Oise. [ . . . ] Despite the role of insurgents that they had usurped, it was vital to get them out of the political realm and back to their natural ranks [ . . . ] the success I enjoyed in this immense task was due to informants.[17]

**6.** Paris is the field of action for the police machine. As is well known, the latter works according to three principles: the repressive principle, the investigative principle and the information principle—from which, of course, the informant and grassing derive. Who is an informant, or *mouton*, in the old carceral jargon? And what does an informant do? How is his work defined? Now—as Richard Cobb has explained[18]—this is precisely his problem: how to make himself recognized as such. At the beginning of his activity, he has to put a lot of effort into being credited as a source. He must accumulate knowledge and reputation, and become specialized. Thus, when the destruction of the archives flings the door open to the informants, the latter, by dint of experience and continuity, will reveal themselves as the true living archives, with their capital of intelligence and their method. If the archive descends and diffuses down among the informants, the police is the medium for this metamorphosis. And if the optimal environment for the informant is the prison, that is indeed where he will outdo himself, seeking to adopt a new role. Here, in direct and constant contact with the police, driven by

17 [Théodore Labourieu?], *Mémoires de M. Claude, chef de la police de sûreté sous le second Empire*, TOME 7 (Paris: Jules Rouff, 1882), pp. 16–17.

18 Richard Cobb, *Police and the People: French Popular Protest, 1789–1820* (Oxford: Oxford University Press, 1970).

their yearning to stand out and persuade, the *moutons* not only construct conspiracies from nothing but also try to endow them with all kinds of distinctive machineries, devices and sundry gadgets; these are 'concealed', that is to say, theatrically exhibited in this site of continuous and perfect inspection, repression and information. Here, when the most accredited tattlers become one and the same with the *agents provocateurs*, the police officers with the informants, when the unlimited demand for intelligence becomes indistinguishable from its inexhaustible supply, amazing zeniths can be reached. Here danger coincides with its signalling, and crime with tipping off, while the act of inspection is always pre-empted by the exhibition of 'evidence'. In these felicitous moments, the police machine is self-generating. Not only because the informant is now ready to enter its ranks. The police in turn will adapt the intelligence it gathers to the authorities for which it is destined, and, like a true informant, its only criterion for the choice of its sources will be the appreciation of its clients, to the point where it will create the intelligence and the events to which that intelligence refers.

The point at which the informant affirms himself fully and tends to outdo himself as *agent provocateur* is also, therefore, the point at which, accordingly, the police becomes able to govern. It will do so in a direct and violent, or in an indirect, diffuse, simulated and subtle way: because when the police fabricates the news, everyday information follows the police model.

But does all this happen in democracy? What has the government of the police to do with the best society and its most harmonious asset? 'And though the police may, in particulars, everywhere appear the same, it cannot finally be denied that their spirit is less devastating where they represent, in absolute monarchy, the power of a ruler in which legislative and executive supremacy are united, than in democracies where their existence, elevated by no such relation, bears witness to the greatest conceivable degeneration of violence.'[19] Walter Benjamin's famous words can be read anew in terms of the unlimited: if democracy is the direct expression of society, it is precisely in democracy that police power knows no limits.

7. The archive can be destroyed without the structure of society being touched; the city, the place of the social par excellence, is not an inert storeroom of news but the living, mobile and unlimited map of crimes. From the streets to the jails and newspapers, it continues its unique and feverish activity; its task is that of reducing crime within the game of social normality. This task is not only aimed at singular persons but at whole *mobs*— or better, at crowds or masses of criminals.

The experience of the *mouton* is better manifested and becomes more fruitful when something unexpected happens. With the sudden eruption of revolt, which interrupts archival continuity, useful and employable informants appear. Yet simultaneously, the crowd—dangerous by definition—suddenly comes to life. The policeman and the *agent provocateur* know better than anybody else that, as Elias Canetti observed in *Masse und Macht*, 'the provoked mass comes together in light of an easily attainable goal'.[20] In the antagonistic game of the crowd, in its

19 Walter Benjamin, 'Critique of Violence' in *Reflections: Essays, Aphorisms, Autobiographical Writings* (Peter Demetz ed., Edmund Jephcott trans.) (New York: Schocken, 1978), p. 287.

20 Elias Canetti, *Crowds and Power* (Carol Stewart trans.) (New York: Continuum, 1973[1960]), p. 49, translation modified (the English translation has 'baiting crowd' for 'provoked mass').

formation as much as in its rapid dissolution, the police continuously recomposes social normality, instituting the undisputed dominance of 'facts'. Paris is the capital of Haussmann and Chief Bertillon;[21] it is the society that advances where the mutinous multitude retreats.

The city really becomes one's own only in the moment of revolt, because only revolt renders the city knowable for a moment. There, and for the first time, one is no longer alone. But when the crowd unravels, society is again one and the same with every one of its walls and streets. Then, the 'one is no longer alone' becomes 'we are again in society'. Once again, the city becomes inappropriable while city planning emerges from the dust of the dispersed mass.

**8.** One has only to think of the problem of collective crime. Scipio Sighele, the author of *La folla delinquente* (*The Criminal Crowd*, 1891), clearly distinguished the crowd from society. No matter how small, each society is akin to what Bentham called a 'permanent political body' and constitutes a space of homogenous and organic relationships between individuals who possess homogenous characteristics. The crowd, on the contrary, 'is a *par excellence heterogeneous* mass of men, as it is composed by individuals of every age, sex, class, social conditions, morality and breeding; and *par excellence inorganic*, as it forms all of a sudden, instantaneously, without any prior agreement'.[22] In the study of these new infrequent and

21 [Alphonse Bertillon (1853–1914), chief of the photographic service of the Paris prefecture. Bertillon pioneered a system for classifying and identifying criminals, and is considered the father of judicial anthropometry; this biometric system came to be popularly referred to as *bertillonage*.]

22 Scipio Sighele, *La folla delinquente* (Clara Gallini ed.) (Venice: Marsilio, 1985[1891]), p. 56.

fleeting 'facts', collective psychology will come to the rescue of sociology.

In the dangerous crowd, a phenomenon suffused by crime, what counts is not so much who leads—the inveterate delinquent, an already familiar subject—but those who are caught up in it, unexpectedly and for the very first time. Sighele thus speaks of the power of suggestion and makes use of analogy with hypnosis (which Freud will define as a 'group formation with two members' [*eine Masse zu zweit*] 20 years later); the French psychiatrist cites the experiences of the Salpêtrière school against the theories of the Nancy school. He draws from Charcot, Gilles de la Tourette, Pitres: '[T]he irresponsibility of hypnotized subjects—the latter argues—is never absolute.'[23] And Sighele can conclude that 'therefore, the *normal ego* [*io normale*] always outlives the *abnormal ego* [*io anormale*] created by the hypnotist [*suggestionatore*]'.[24] Even though the crowd is not society, and even though sociology has to give way to social psychology, the expulsion from the social is never complete. And it is the pathological phenomenon, which seems to escape the viewpoint of the sociologist, that enables, through mass psychology, the correction and limitless evolution of that viewpoint.

If social individuality persists in the recesses of the psyche, revolt is bound to end, it seems, just as the apparently uncontrollable horde will be soon normalized. Despite being occasionally dragged into the uprising, in its intimate core the individual will never cease to be *sociable*. Paris reorganizes itself as such in the disorganized crowd, it stalks it with its shadow, forces it to flee and—around every street corner, inside every

23 Ibid., p. 109.
24 Ibid., p. 113.

doorway and hiding place—it captures individual psyches, bringing them back to the organic evolution of society.

9. 'The workers,' the revolutionary socialist Hubert Lagardelle observed, 'understand perfectly well that the bourgeois defend the fatherland, but they think of themselves as standing outside of it. This conviction may scandalize us, but it's a fact . . . .'

'All illnesses,' Durkheim answered smiling, 'are facts.' [25]

Whether normal or pathological, every 'fact', however, answers to a complex dynamic. There are of course subjects that obey a normal system of collective representations: their normality is completely social and (like the corresponding pathology) it concerns sociology directly. But the social character of the pathological is not a norm or an axiom. Some subjects are in fact ill, or, better, abnormal, precisely because they are incapable of reaching a shared level of representations. *La Conscience morbide* was the title chosen in 1914 by Charles Blondel, and it is the name of this entirely subjective impossibility, of this painful incapacity to share socially: after all, as the study of visions and irrational behaviour demonstrates, mental illness hailed from a separation, from a precise loss, from the end of contact between the individual and his group or *milieu*. In the 1920s, while Marcel Mauss brings new light to Durkheim's theory and elaborates the notion of the 'total social fact', the psychiatrist Blondel reads [Henri] Bergson, William James and especially [Lucien]

25 Émile Durkheim, 'Internationalisme et lutte des classes' (1906) in *La science sociale et l'action* (Paris: PUF, 2010), p. 288.

Lévy-Bruhl. In keeping with the theory of collective representations, he discovers the planet of *total consciousness*
[*conscience totale*] and its two faces: the luminous one, in
which the common elements are grouped together, 'capable of being expressed in words defined by collective
experience and translated into actions regulated by the
group';[26] and the other, the dark and fathomless domain
of internal sensation, 'of an exclusively individual experience',[27] of the life without words that vacillates with its
strange non-facts between corporeal intimacy and 'what
is purely psychological'.[28] According to Blondel, in order
for a normal consciousness to be established, a process
of 'decanting' must take place at the centre of 'total consciousness': the sum of shared representations must
come to light and prevail over internal sensations, over
the *masse cénesthésique*, the kinaesthetic mass that can
thus sediment itself in the subconscious. The pure psychological aspect is thereby delimited and translated into
collective representations; only then can psychic life
exceed the impenetrable barriers of individuality and
make its legitimate entry, expressing and deploying itself
in the *social milieu*.

If, however, the delicate mechanism is halted, if
something upsets or impedes the process of decantation,
the *conscience claire* (clear consciousness) becomes
directly invested by the *inaccoutumées* (unaccustomed)
components of the psyche, *anormalement irréductibles*
(abnormally irreducible) to the sociality of the world and
of language. What we have then is the manifestation

26 Charles Blondel, *The Troubled Conscience and the Insane Mind*
(F. G. Crookshank ed.) (London: Kegan Paul, Trench, Trübner,
1928), p. 53.
27 Ibid., p. 48.
28 Ibid., p. 63.

of mental illness with its agonizing disorder and the now-unchallenged din of its enigmatic voices. Of course, the subject has not suddenly lost the ability to speak, but language, the social fact par excellence, no longer has any grips on his condition. He struggles along while the incommunicable laps against language within him, giving rise to the incongruous. It's the sign, Blondel says, 'of an authentic psychic anarchy, of an authentic revolt of individual consciousness against collective dispositions'.[29]

10. The word 'anarchy' makes its appearance here. Not by chance, for sure—but what does it mean? Among a thousand possible examples, two: In his *Suggestion und Hypnotismus in der Völkerpsychologie* (1894), the great Zurich ethnologist Otto Stoll disagrees with the Lombroso of *L'uomo delinquente* (*Criminal Man*) and interprets anarchist action as the response to an acute hallucinatory state. For Stoll, the bomber is not a born criminal. A typical subject of mass political suggestion, he is actually an ordinary young person who falls victim to a crisis as temporary as it is irrepressible. Pulled along by 'the libertarian saints or the prophets of socialism',[30] he will soon go from a state of frenzied excitement to a 'homicidal ecstasy' (*Mordekstase*),[31] tragically turning the visions of the doctrine, the shining phantoms of propaganda, into a conclusive act. Even the hypnotic power that guides his hand stems from an illusion. One wave

29 Charles Blondel, *La conscience morbide. Essai de psychopathologie générale, 2e édition augmentée d'un appendice* (Paris: Félix Alcan, 1928), p. 292.

30 Otto Stoll, *Suggestion und Hypnotismus in der Völkerpsychologie* (Leipizig: Veit, 1904[1894]), pp. 579–80.

31 Ibid., p. 579.

follows another, and behind suggestion there lies a suggestion more ancient and powerful.

In 1909, Otto Rank publishes his study on the myth
of the birth of the hero (*Der Mythos von der Geburt des
Helden*). This famous text, which samples some pages
from Freud, concludes with an allusion to the antisocial
figure par excellence, 'the anarchist'. Rank observes that
if only one recognized his affinity with the hero of myths,
namely the psychological conflict which every heroic
mythology stages with noticeably constant features, even
the regicide assassin could be spared the most severe
punishments; if only it was recognized that his 'morbid
trait . . . is the pathologic transference of the hatred from
the father to the real king', and that in fact he 'has killed
an entirely different person from the one he really
intended to destroy',[32] such a man could be kept from the
gallows.

Blondel's position is diametrically opposed. In
Blondel, 'anarchy' carries the most complete opposition
to the Freudian project. As he combatively argues against
psychoanalysis, 'the more it becomes intelligible to us,
the more mental disorder loses all appearance of mor-
bidity, if not in its consequences then at least—which is
essential—in its mechanism.'[33] If the *psychologique
pur* can termed such, it is exactly because it cannot be
interpreted. The attention of the scholar must therefore
shift from this initial sedimentation to a slightly higher
but not yet sociologically intermediate level, at the 'centre'
of the total consciousness. And if Sighele saw in the

32 Otto Rank, *The Myth of the Birth of the Hero: A Psychological
Interpretation of Mythology* (F. Robbins and Smith Ely Jelliffe trans)
(New York: The Journal of Nervous and Mental Disease, 1914),
p. 94.

33 Blondel, *La conscience morbide*, p. 382.

individual psyche the last line of defence against the power of suggestion, an inalienable residue of the social, for Blondel this ostensible residue hides a real *dispositif.* For him, everything is staked on this. So much so that in his framework, the sphere of 'social facts' corresponds to the correct functioning of consciousness. Indeed, in order to be able to enact within itself the already sociological opposition between healthy and unhealthy, the social itself had to constitute itself as normal. And this is what happens when the 'decantation' takes place: then the individual is both normal and social, and the social becomes normal within him.

And if the subject who disobeys a system of collective representations will thus appears as abnormal, asocial and anarchic, this is not due to a repressed ancient conflict but because the function of the unlimited is now operative at the centre of his consciousness.


11. *Les foules ne sont pas seulement crédules, elles sont folles* (The masses are not just credulous, they're mad). As Gabriel Tarde observes, absolute absence of moderation, intolerance, hypertrophic pride, a continuous oscillation between the extremes of excitement and depression, furious eroticism and stupefying panic—these are the features common to the alienated and to crowds. Like the former, crowds too suffer from hallucinations. His beloved Taine nicely reminds us of this in a passage from his *La Révolution* [The Revolution], which Tarde evokes in his chapter on the 'Le Public et la foule' (The Public and the Crowd) (1898). At the end of July 1789, driven by the general excitement, a rumour spreads in the provinces of Angoumois, Périgord and Auvergne: '[T]en thousand, twenty thousand brigands had arrived—they had been seen, their dust rising in the distant horizon,

coming to massacre everyone.'[34] And then everyone flees, abandoning their homes in haste and spending the night hiding in the forests scared. Until dawn reveals that the danger was only imaginary, a bad daydream; by now it has passed and people can return calmly to their villages. But it is precisely then that the collective delirium bursts forth. That morbid feeling of anxiety, the panic about a murderous mob that had gathered together a helpless crowd and forced it to flee, had to be justified somehow; it demanded some kind of satisfaction—as a rumour suggests: 'If the danger doesn't come in the form of brigands, it is coming from somewhere else.'[35] *D'ailleurs* (from somewhere else), Tarde explains, meaning from supposed conspirators. So, the defenceless fugitives turn into implacable hunters, panicked paralysis into murderous excitement; and the fantastical danger gives rise to all-too-real persecutions.

In order for this inversion to take place, however, a difference must emerge—someone in the group must rise above the others, an idea must attract attention. This is how crowds come alive . . . . By chance an idea appears, in the guise of an elementary syllogism, which in its various versions will become canonical. Partially veiled but not at all disconfirmed by the first rumour, the proposition *le peril vient* (the danger is coming) is rediscovered. The first lights could not dispel it and evidence is not enough to contradict it because it does not ask for something to become apparent but stubbornly points to the invisible; it teaches that true danger never stops coming,

---

34 Gabriel Tarde, 'Conviction and the Crowd', *Distinktion: Journal of Social Theory* 14(2) (2013): 236; Gabriel Tarde, 'Le Public et la foule' (1898) in *L'Opinion et la foule* (Paris: PUF, 1989[1901]), p. 67.
35 Tarde, 'Le Public et la foule', p. 67.

and that it will thus also be the vaguest danger, the one we can only surmise.

The idea is a cheap one. But what matters is that a legion of *menés* (the led) appropriates it, following its *meneur* (leader). In fact, though he is sometimes hidden, the crowd *must* always have a leader. Of course, 'it often happens that a crowd set in motion by a clique of zealots will outstrip and assimilate them and, having become acephalous, it will appear to be devoid of leaders. The truth is that it no longer has leaders, just as leavened dough no longer contains any yeast.' There would be no crowds without leaders because no follower 'invents anything', because they are unable to develop, remaining both dumb and short-lived. As is now obvious, it is not that crowds have shown themselves to be so receptive to conceptions based on fate and a mastery of the elements. Completely ephemeral as they are, crowds are fascinated by the idea of eternal existence, which they will always call upon, explicitly or otherwise. In this way, it is not history but pure and mythic 'nature' that acts in them. Tarde too had highlighted this, distinguishing them from more evolved social forms:

> There is something animalistic about the crowd. Is it not a bundle of psychic contagions essentially produced by physical contacts? But no other communication from mind to mind, from soul to soul, has the proximity of bodies as its necessary condition [ . . . ]. The crowd, as a more natural grouping, is the most subjected to the forces of nature; it depends on rain or sunshine, hot or cold weather; it is more frequent in summer than winter. A ray of light brings it together; a downpour disperses it.[36]

36 Ibid., p. 39.

We recognize here an implicit quotation in Canetti's later text, 'Rain is the crowd in the moment of discharge, and stands also for its disintegration. The clouds whence it comes dissolve into rain; the drops fall because they can keep together no longer, and it is not clear whether, or when, they can coalesce again.'[37]

But where does this transitory character of the crowd come from? We could suppose the emergence of another figure, even if in a farcical and worn-out form, in the crowd's revolt. We could think as much if we recall a well-known passage: 'Bourgeois revolutions, like those of the eighteenth century, storm swiftly from success to success, their dramatic effects outdo each other, men and things seem set in sparkling brilliants, ecstasy is the everyday spirit, but they are short-lived, soon they have attained their zenith, and a long crapulent depression seizes society'.[38]

12. In the meantime, Paris reorganizes itself.

Marcel Poëte was the first from the French school to show that the City is a living being endowed with a collective soul [ . . . ] and its own behaviour. Now that we know this living being as a localized unit (albeit a moving one) in continuous interaction with the other social units, localized or otherwise, differing in volume and density, that are scattered across geographical extension, one can affirm, as Durkheim does, that this unit comprises an *individual* being,

37 Canetti, *Crowds and Power*, p. 82.

38 Karl Marx, 'The Eighteenth Brumaire of Louis Bonaparte' in Karl Marx and Friedrich Engels, *Collected Works, Volume 11: Marx and Engels, 1851–1853* (London: Lawrence & Wishart, 1979), p. 106.

which sinks its roots in the urban site, and a *social* being, which is constantly immersed in the broader civilization. From their reciprocal exchanges is born the general behaviour of that being we call the city.[39]

So concludes Gaston Bardet in his *Problèmes d'urbanisme* [Problems of Urbanization]. Paris has given rise to its own vision, called 'urbanism', in constant contact with the sciences that mark the social domain—disciplines that now appear, in the words of Pierre Lavedan, 'diverse and yet cohesive'.[40]

Both typical and banal, the urbanist is a subject attracted to the enduring mirage of social progress. 'Preoccupied with the current fate of the city, he will project this fate back into the past, to the time of its birth'.[41] For him, urban history will therefore be nothing other than the movement of society towards itself and the law of this evolution will coincide (as 'fate' would have it) with his own good work. 'The sense of urban life in all its complexity is indispensable to him. Just as the doctor gathers information about his patient's history, he must learn that of the city.'[42]

**13.** 'The city is much more than a simple manifestation of life; it is also one of its forms,' Poëte again affirms.[43]

39 Gaston Bardet, *Problèmes d'urbanisme* (Paris: Dunod, 1948), p. 10.

40 Pierre Lavedan, *Qu' est-ce que l'Urbanisme? Introduction à l'Histoire de l'Urbanisme* (Paris: Laurens, 1926), p. 1.

41 Marcel Poëte, 'L'Évolution des villes', *La Vie urbaine* 5 (1930): 299.

42 Ibid.: 298.

43 Marcel Poëte, 'Paris. Son évolution créatrice, I. Introduction à la vie urbaine', *La Vie urbaine* 40 (1937): 197.

And as Bardet observes, 'starting from different disciplines, both the biologist Patrick Geddes and then the
sociologist Victor Deznài arrived at similar conclusions.'[44]

According to Deznài, in the sociology of the city the
genitive becomes subjective. For him, the city must equip
itself with its own social knowledge, coordinating the various administrations, meaning the centres of its 'intellectual activity'. The latter also includes the training of
urbanists themselves. Intellectually vital cities will thus
establish 'in their defence and to perfect their organization' their offices 'of urban studies, where the theoretical
and practical Science of the City will be fostered'.[45] The
task envisaged by Deznài thus involves something like a
constant reflection: society folds back on itself, just as the
city moves towards itself, while urbanism models and
regulates its own disciplinary figure, in a movement that
in fact corresponds exactly to the advancing of crowds.

> The intellectual activity of the city must [ . . . ]
> especially take into consideration the increased
> importance of urban *crowds*, and try to acquire a
> spiritual influence over them. This is why all the
> intellectual activities of the city will necessarily
> have an educational character vis-à-vis the huge
> masses of inhabitants, which it is necessary to
> transform into citizens conscious of the high
> quality of city planning, possessing a general
> culture, filled with a profound social sensitivity.
> [ . . . ] The current fight for internal equilibrium
> and urban security cannot be successful unless

44 Bardet, *Problèmes d'urbanisme*, p. 9n9.

45 Victor Deznài, 'L'activité intellectuelle des villes', *Urbanismul*
14(11–12) (1936): 525.

it is carried out with the weapons of intelligence
by a conscientious urban spirit.[46]

In this way, if every ideal of government has to yield
to that of society, not even the central state can remain
as the paradigm of the new political organization: it is
too heterogeneous, while the unlimited requires its own
specific technique which, rigorously complying with the
primacy of the sociological, comes from the city and
returns to it. 'The visible and overpowering evolution that
leads to *the complete urbanization of the state* is already
being realized, as we can only hope. This,' Deznài concludes, 'will be at the same time an economic, construc-
tive and peaceful organism; it will be governed by reason
and only called upon to coordinate the activity of the
urban elements that compose it.'[47]

Society thus prevails over discipline while remaining
indifferent towards restricted limits and demanding—
always in the name of the unlimited—the most direct
incarnation: the statesman or the state *tout court*, the
state, that is to say man *tout court*, will be a physician or,
better, a sociologist or, better yet, a democratic urbanist.

Paris thus reorganizes itself by individualizing the
crowd: by dispersing and thereby disseminating itself in
the suburbs and remodelling itself on the basis of
this dissemination, it moulds, by a kind of feedback
effect, its own concentrated form on that of the isolated
cells in the mass suburbs that had been produced by spatial detachment. Urbanism works on the natural functions of the crowd and because it assures the fulfilment
of its needs under all circumstances, it disperses and
maintains it, protects and diffuses it in a single gesture.

---

46 Ibid.: 526.

47 Ibid.

This is why—in the words of Lewis Mumford in *The City in History*—its ideal is always and everywhere 'an encapsulated life'. This is also why those individuals who, finally equipped with 'a profound communal sensitivity', willingly accept this kind of existence 'might as well be encased in a rocket hurtling through space'. It is with them that a new form of life appears; it is here, in unlimited urbanization, that 'we find *The Lonely Crowd*'.[48]

**14.** 'No one today will believe your prophecies': these are the words with which the publisher [Pierre-Jules] Hetzel refuses Jules Verne's *Paris au XX^e siècle*. It was the end of 1863. Reading only the first chapter on the Instructional Credit Union, the organism (a hybrid of bank and enterprise) that looks after the ridiculously technical education that holds sway in this capital of 1960, it would be rather easy to remark that the bad prophet was really Hetzel, or whoever Hetzel thought he represented, while Verne's vision sharply delineated the subsequent epoch and his humour was able to capture its more unconscious and grotesque character. But that was not where Hetzel's error really lay. He was mistaken because the novel's principle and its greatness is not at all to be found in its prophetic character.

Consider the solemn as well as comic moment of the great annual ceremony in which the union awards the most deserving students. The head of Applied Sciences delivers his speech: he speaks with pitying contempt of the Paris of 1860 and of the small France of the

---

48 Lewis Mumford, *The City in History: Its Origins, Its Transformations, and Its Prospects* (New York: Harcourt, Brace and World, 1961), p. 512. ['The Lonely Crowd' is the title of a famous sociological essay published by David Riesman, with Nathan Glazer and Reuel Denney, in 1950.]

nineteenth century, enumerating instead with rhetorical elan the most recent wonders of technology, the speed of communication and transport and the virtues of home energy supply. In this, he was 'sublime, lyrical, dithyrambic; in short quite intolerable and unjust, forgetting that the wonders of his century were already germinating in the projects of its predecessor'.[49] What Verne ironically expounds and lays claim to here is precisely the generative principle of the novel. It is not a matter of a more or less credible or successful prophecy but, once more, of the unlimited. The condition of possibility of science-fiction discourse, of the science-fiction novel in 1860, is that the capital of the nineteenth century knows no limits: nothing will escape today or tomorrow, and the Paris of 1860 with its boulevards contains not only the past but also the predictable schema of the seasons to come. The *être urbain* (urban being) named Paris is not only 'made of the past', as Poëte said—it does not just 'put all of its past, en bloc, at the service of the creation of the present'[50] but also its future. Of course, as Gertrude Stein observed in 'Portraits and Repetition', in Verne, everything is 'terribly real terribly near but still not here'.[51] But this very phrase betrays an impatience and draws everything towards itself: here it is terrible that even the 'still not' is real and near.

For Verne, there is the novel, the adventure of the young Michel Dufrénoy through the vast, lit streets and the fast underground trains, 200 instruments playing in unison in the *concert électrique* and an electric discharge

49 Jules Verne, *Paris in the Twentieth Century* (Richard Howard trans.) (New York: Ballantine, 1996), p. 12.

50 Poëte, 'Paris. Son évolution créatrice, I': 212.

51 Gertrude Stein, 'Portraits and Repetition' in *Writings, 1932–1936* (New York: Library of America, 1998), p. 289.

that has replaced the guillotine—there is all of this because there is no future that can deny itself to an unlimited present.

Science fiction and progressivism were born together. The former, however, under the guise of fabulation, grasps the real principle of the present, which remains unknown to the latter, for all its show of seriousness.

For the unlimited is a dream. And the fact that this dream governs—to the point that a fantastic story appears as an accurate prophecy—does not contradict its oneiric character.

Between December 1960 and January 1961, Antonio Delfini gains his insight: Stendhal's imagined Chartreuse is the Abbey of Nonantola; the estates of Parma are the estates of Este; the Po is the Po and the Austrian states are the Austrian or pontifical states, while the villa of Sanseverina is the Cataio on Euganean hills 'where the duke of Modena kept Ciro Menotti in chains for almost two months': because Fabrizio Del Dongo is none other than Menotti and Clelia Conti is Rosa Giavarina Rodeschein as well as Moreali, Menotti's wife; and the bells of Steccata are those of the church of Carmine in Modena. When Delfini writes *Modena 1831. Città della Chartreuse*, he discovers that, in the unlimited, Modena can become Parma just as it could become New York; more, it must become Parma and remain hidden beneath Parma's foundations for 130 years, held fast by Parma's aura. '*Parme* would be the conclusive result of the dream. From Parma [ . . . ] we will not strip the sound of the word which is altogether different from the sound of the word Modena.'[52] But the unlimited is a dream just

---

52 Antonio Delfini, *Modena 1831. Città della Chartreuse* (Milan: Libri Schweiller, 1993[1962]), p. 40.

as 'The Chartreuse is the dream of Moreali, dreamt again and transcribed by Stendhal.'[53] For 'Stendhal dreams of dreaming for her. And the dreams are transferred, they do not gather in the place or places that reality would have wished for.'[54] In Rome in 1960, Delfini discovers another dream of the nineteenth century in Stendhal's dream, just as Stendhal's dream had done in the dream of the unlimited: he discovers Modena and the Carbonari revolts and Menotti and the ignominy of the duke, and in background colouring of the unlimited he finds the slight, irreducible folds that free reality as the dream within the dream, and in the city liberate revolt from the faded scars of its failure.

15. The dream of the world dreaming itself always harbours the dream of the world's or the crowd's immense goodness. In 1913, a book entitled Crowds: A Moving-Picture of Democracy graces bookshop displays; it is a bestseller in New York. Gerald Stanley Lee, the New England preacher, has left his old pulpit behind and converted to the optimism of progress, pouring out his new faith in chapters with ringing titles ('Letting the Crowd Be Good', 'Letting the Crowd Be Beautiful', 'Crowd and Heroes'): 'I have known and faced [ . . . ] the Crowd Fear. I know in some dogged, submerged, and speechless way that it is not a true fear.'[55] A euphoric horde of small businessmen admires his glorious vision, following it from page to page: they satisfy but also revive their aspirations in its vague reflections, recognizing themselves as equipped with 'a new and extraordinary

---

53 Ibid., p. 47.

54 Ibid.

55 Gerald Stanley Lee, Crowds: A Moving-Picture of Democracy (Garden City, NY: Doubleday, Page, 1913), p. 32.

sense of the invisible',[56] with the most marked 'sense of what is going to happen next in the world'.[57] According to Lee, the imaginative power of crowds, that is, the work of a boundless mass of fervid imaginations, grasps the future, making it present; everything is already here now and that is why it is beautifully real: 'Imagination about the future is going to make the next few hundred years an organic part of every man's life to-day.'[58] This is the enormous undertaking, the magic expectation or the performative wisdom of the collective dream *that makes things happen*: all the inventions to come are thus brought together in the current invention of a 'new kind and new size of human being',[59] a welter of creatives capable of holding fast to their fantasies and producing affluence with the purest desire as their sole material. As a counterbalance to fear, hope is indeed now 'the only way to see through things'.[60] If the future is in fact the good or possibility as such, all possible goodness becomes real in everyone's imagination; in the one who hopes, today becomes tomorrow, the impossible possible, while goodness is spread and affirmed. 'I have seen that being good is the one great adventure of the world, the huge daily passionate moral experiment of the human heart—that all men are at work on it, that goodness is an implacable crowd process, and that nothing can stop it.'[61] These are the final lines of the chapter entitled 'Goodness as a Crowd-Process'. From what at first sight may appear as

56 Ibid., p. 64.

57 Ibid.

58 Ibid.

59 Ibid., p. 62.

60 Ibid., p. 87.

61 Ibid., p. 115.

curious convolutions, it is clear how, in Lee's vision and other more current misapprehensions, the idea of the goodness of the multitudes sets off the process of the production of the crowd. It will then also be possible to see how, while it dreamt its own goodness in pompous phrases, the world had long been dreaming the crowd; that long before now and even before 1913, the world possessed, in the common name 'democracy', the dream of an implacable crowd, of which—as it was once said—it must only acquire the consciousness.

16. Perhaps developing the ideas of Theodor Geiger ('Panik im Mittelstand' [Panic in the Middle Classes, 1930])[62] about the petty bourgeoisie as a non-class or a simple grouping (*Bevölkerungsblock*) of the two antagonistic classes, and on Nazism as petty-bourgeois panic, Walter Benjamin wrote, in note appended to his essay on 'The Work of Art in the Age of Its Technological Reproducibility':

> The mass as an impenetrable, compact entity, which Le Bon and others have made the subject of their 'mass psychology' is that of the petty bourgeoisie. The petty bourgeoisie is not a class; it is in fact only a mass. And the greater the pressure acting on it between the two antagonistic classes of the bourgeoisie and the proletariat, the more compact it becomes. In *this* mass, the emotional element described in mass psychology is indeed a determining factor. [ . . . ] Demonstrations by the compact mass thus always have a panicked quality—whether they

---

62 Theodor Geiger, 'Panik in Mittelstand', *Die Arbeit. Zeitschrift für Gewerkschaftspolitik und Wirtschaftskunde* 10 (1930): 637–54.

give vent to war fever, hatred of Jews, or the instinct for self-preservation.[63]

For our purposes, this note—which [Theodor W.] Adorno defines as the most profound and powerful thing he had read in the domain of political theory after [Lenin's] *State and Revolution*—contains a fundamental precept; for it is still this cohesive mass that society normalizes. Taking possession of the city again will thus mean, in the sense suggested by Benjamin, isolating and distinguishing the revolutionary class from the crowd, so that the former 'ceases to be governed by mere reactions'.[64] The distinction is not purely theoretical: in it lies the possibility of a loosening (*Auflockerung*), of antagonisms capable of disactivating the social *dispositif*. The model for this loosening was offered by Marx in the final pages of *The Poverty of Philosophy* (1847), from which Benjamin seems to draw inspiration, as he opposes revolutionary solidarity to the reactive conduct of the petty bourgeoisie: the constitution of the working class into a cohesive, solidary class is for Marx 'a veritable civil war' in which 'all the elements necessary for a coming battle unite and develop'.[65]

A society in which (quoting Benjamin again) 'neither the objective nor the subjective conditions for the formation of masses will exist'[66] will no longer be unlimited; in it, even the sociological fact par excellence, which dictates the rules of normalization, stops being a 'fact'. Only

63 Walter Benjamin, 'The Work of Art in the Age of Its Technological Reproducibility (Second Version)' in *Selected Writings, Volume 3, 1935–1938* (Howard Eiland and Michael W. Jennings eds) (Cambridge, MA: Belknap Press, 2002), p. 129.

64 Ibid.

65 Marx, *The Poverty of Philosophy*, p. 211.

66 Benjamin, 'The Work of Art', p. 129.

then, at the end of the struggle, will we be able truly to appropriate the city, and the city will no longer be itself.

**17.** Benjamin's note begins like this:

> [P]roletarian class consciousness [*Das prole-tarische Klassenbewusstsein*], which is the most enlightened form of class consciousness, fundamentally transforms the structure of the proletarian masses. The class-conscious proletariat forms a compact mass only from the outside, in the minds of its oppressors. At the moment when it takes up its struggle for liberation, this apparently compact mass has actually already begun to loosen. It ceases to be governed by mere reactions; it makes the transition to action. The loosening of the proletarian masses is the work of solidarity [*Solidarität*]. In the solidarity of the proletarian class struggle, the dead, undialectical opposition between individual and mass is abolished; for the comrade, it does not exist. Decisive as the masses are for the revolutionary leader, therefore, his great achievement lies not in drawing the masses after him, but in constantly incorporating himself into the masses, in order to be, for them, always one among hundreds of thousands.[67]

As in Freud—whose *Massenpsychologie und Ich-Analyse* (*Group Psychology and the Analysis of the Ego*) was written in 1921—mass (*Masse*) here means 'crowd'; in a preparatory variant of the note (Ms 988)[68] Benjamin too,

---

67 Ibid.

68 Walter Benjamin, *Gesammelte Schriften VII.2* (Rolf Tiedemann and Hermann Schweppenhauser eds) (Frankfurt: Suhrkamp, 1991), p. 668.

like Freud, cites the title of Le Bon's *La Psychologie des foules* in Rudolf Eisler's German translation: *Psychologie der Massen*. Of course, in the course of his treatise, Freud also distinguishes *Masse*, in the sense of artificial, organized and stable masses (army and church), from *Haufen*, which is equivalent to the English 'crowd' and designates it as a transitory phenomenon in the sense of Sighele and Le Bon. Now, though this distinction does not take on a fundamental significance in Freud's text, in Benjamin's, it does not appear at all. But in Benjamin, *Masse* does not just mean 'crowd' (*Menge*, or even *Mass als solche*, 'mass as such', in *The Arcades Project*); it can extend its purview, touching on two different and diametrically opposed meanings: it can compress itself and become the dangerous compact petty-bourgeois crowd or dilate into the revolutionary class. *Il y toujours une carte variable des masses sous la reproduction des classes* (There is always a variable map of the masses beneath the reproduction of classes). For Benjamin, *Masse* is already a dynamic term.

Equally obvious, from the initial lines of the note (*Das proletarische Klassenbewusstesein*), is Benjamin's reference to [Georg] Lukács. *Geshichte und Klassenbewusstesein* (*History and Class Consciousness*, 1923) was a very important book for Benjamin too, who read it under the advice of Ernst Bloch. In Lukács' book, we find the following assertion: '[C]lass consciousness is identical with neither the psychological consciousness of individual members of the proletariat, nor with the (mass-psychological) consciousness of the proletariat as a whole; but it is, on the contrary, *the sense, become conscious, of the historical role of the class.*'[69] For Benjamin, it was this

69 Georg Lukács, *History and Class Consciousness: Studies in Marxist Dialectics* (Rodney Livingstone trans.) (Cambridge, MA: The MIT Press, 1971), p. 73.

consciousness of the historical situation that makes possible a transformation of the mass, its loosening. But this loosening is also the product of solidarity. Proletarian class consciousness and solidarity are indistinguishable. Solidarity is not what it usually appears to be, namely, a good Christian feeling. It is a structural modification, internal to the mass, which, by transforming the sociological into the political, the proletariat into the revolutionary class, only seems to leave the mass unchanged, letting it appear as compact only to the external observer, the one not in solidarity, the oppressor. Where there is solidarity—a solidarity that cannot come from the outside, that no one can be expected to bring—that is, when the bonds of antagonism are broken, only then is there class consciousness (the reverse is also true). When there is no solidarity or consciousness, there is no class; there is only the petty-bourgeois mass, with its well-behaved psychology.

Reviewing Brecht's play *Die Mutter* (*The Mother*) in 1932, Benjamin noted how the mother moved from helping her son, 'from the first kind of help', 'to the ultimate, the solidarity of the working class'.[70] With regard to this example of revolutionary praxis, he observed: 'It is in the nature of epic theatre to replace the undialectical opposition between the form and content of consciousness (which means that a character can only refer to his own actions by reflexions) by the dialectical one between theory and praxis (which means that any action that makes a breakthrough opens up a clearer view of theory).'[71]

---

70 Walter Benjamin, 'A Family Drama in the Epic Theatre' in *Understanding Brecht* (Anna Bostock trans.) (London: Verso, 1998), p. 35.
71 Ibid.

The adialectical contraposition between individual and mass here appears as a contraposition between the form and the content of consciousness.

If the domain of these two kinds of contrast is the mass, class theory does not arise from reflection but from action, and theory is nothing but a dialectical stage of praxis. Class is therefore not a compact mass, just like the theory of the revolutionary class is not psychology. The true object of social psychology is the dangerous crowd: with a 'Frankfurtian' turn of phrase, we could say here that 'the irrationality of the object of observation merges with the irrationality of the observer'. Instead, the theory of the revolutionary class is itself revolutionary: it frees itself from action while freeing it in turn.

18. Class consciousness has no contents and is not reflexive. This means that it is not the 'psychological consciousness of individual members of the proletariat'. How did Benjamin understand these words by Lukács? Revolutionary consciousness could not be the consciousness of an ego for him either.

The false distinction between form and content, in fact, depends on another distinction, the one that first separates and then joins back knowledge and experience. 'This notion,' as Benjamin had already written in 1918 ('Über das Programm der kommenden Philosophie'),

> is, however, mythology, and so far as its truth content is concerned, it is the same as every other epistemological mythology. We know of primitive peoples of the so-called preanimistic stage who identify themselves with sacred animals and plants and name themselves after them; we know of insane people who likewise

also identify themselves in part with objects of their perception [ . . . ] we know of sick people who relate the sensations of their bodies not to themselves but rather to other creatures. [ . . . ] The commonly shared notions of sensuous (and intellectual) knowledge in our epoch, as well as in the Kantian and the pre-Kantian epochs, is very much a mythology like those mentioned. [ . . . ] Cognizing man, the cognizing empirical consciousness is a type of insane consciousness. This means nothing more than that within empirical consciousness there are only gradual differences among its various types.[72]

Many years later, Benjamin reprises these youthful pages. In the fragment K 1,4 of the *Arcades Project*, he describes the nineteenth century as a 'period' (*Zeitraum*) that is also a collective 'dreamtime' (*Zeit-Traum*). The consolidation of individual consciousness through reflection is accompanied here by the collapse of collective consciousness in the oneiric world. In the subsequent fragment, this epochal *dispositif* is referred back to the dynamics of empirical consciousness which, with reference to Freud, is now described in very similar terms to those of 1918. 'It is one of the tacit suppositions of psychoanalysis that the clear-cut antithesis of sleeping and waking has no value for determining the empirical form of consciousness of the human being, but instead yields before an unending variety of concrete states of consciousness conditioned by every conceivable level of

---

72 Walter Benjamin, 'On the Program of the Coming Philosophy' in *Selected Writings, Volume 1, 1913–1926* (Marcus Bullock and Michael W. Jennings eds) (Cambridge, MA: Harvard University Press, 1996), pp. 103–4.

wakefulness within all possible centers.'[73] In the modern mythological context, the reflection with which consciousness asserts itself at an individual level represents a degree of the same infinite spectrum that, at a collective level, delirious consciousness traverses in dream.

> Of course, much that is external to the [individual] is internal to the [collective]: architecture, fashion—yes, even the weather—are, in the interior of the collective, what the sensoria of organs, the feeling of sickness or health, are inside the individual. And so long as they preserve this unconscious, amorphous dream configuration, they are as much natural processes as digestion, breathing, and the like.[74]

This last phrase sounds like an inversion (between the external and the internal, the individual and the collective) of the one which in the early writing defined the delirious consciousness: '[W]e know of sick people who relate the sensations of their bodies not to themselves but rather to other creatures.' Every phenomenon truly external to the individual now appears internal to the dreaming body of Paris while the conscious ego with its reflections, experiences and psychological contents is revealed to be an ever-darker lost recess in the great sleeping crowd.

Introducing the concept of intentional consciousness, as 'reference to a content', 'direction towards an object' (*Richtung auf ein Objekt*), Franz Brentano employed the term 'fusion', thereby indicating that in the psychic act

---

73 Walter Benjamin, *The Arcades Project* (Howard Eiland and Kevin McLaughlin trans) (Cambridge, MA: Harvard University Press, 1999), p. 389.

74 Ibid., pp. 389–90.

CLASS | 41

the poles of object and subject come together in a 'peculiar interweaving' (*eigentümliche Verwebung*); it is precisely this extremely close relation which testifies to the fact that they do not neutralize or blur into each other. Benjamin, who in *Ursprung des deutschen Trauerspiels* (*The Origin of German Tragic Drama*, 1928) will talk of truth as 'death of *intentio*', wrote in 1918: '[A]ll genuine experience rests upon the pure "epistemological (transcendental) consciousness", if this term is still usable under the condition that it be stripped of everything subjective. [ . . . ] The task of future epistemology is to find for knowledge the sphere of total neutrality [*die Sphäre totaler Neutralität*] in regard to the concepts of both subject and object.'[75]

If, according to Marx's letter to [Arnold] Ruge (1843), 'the reform of consciousness consists *entirely* in [ . . . ] arousing [the world] from its dream of itself',[76] it must also lead the false oppositions between internal and external, individual and collective, to a threshold of neutrality.

**19.** 'The materialist presentation of history leads the past to bring the present into a critical state.'[77] It is in formulas such as this (from section N of *The Arcades Project*) that the programme sketched out by the young Benjamin finds its true realization. The term 'present' does not designate here the position from which the 'subject' exercises a more or less detached domination over the past, conceived as a remote and thus isolated object.

75 Benjamin, 'On the Program of the Coming Philosophy', p. 104.

76 Karl Marx, 'Letter to Arnold Ruge, Kreuznach, September 1893' in *Early Writings* (Rodney Livingstone and Gregory Benton trans.) (Harmondsworth: Penguin, 1974), p. 209.

77 Benjamin, *The Arcades Project*, p. 471.

What's more, in this way, the past itself does not know the present. It is not a matter of a simple reversal, but of the collapse of any relation, that is, of all temporal continuity. There is no *continuum*—a well-known motif. What 'now' (*jetzt*) becomes 'knowable' (*erkennbar*) was not known before nor will it ever be again. Only in this 'now' do subject and object finally become neutral, while in the names of 'constellation' (*Konstellation*) and 'dialectical image' (*dialektisches Bild*), Benjamin captures the polarization of an identity into its 'pre- and post-history' (*Vor-und Nachgeschichte*). A polarization—no longer an 'interweaving'—which is also expressed in the formula: 'The subject of historical knowledge is the struggling, oppressed class itself.'[78]

The note on class can be interpreted as a document of this 'materialist presentation'. Its most genuine character, in fact, shines through not so much in the use of terms such as 'class consciousness', 'solidarity', 'proletarian' but especially in the way that Benjamin takes up the position of the old bourgeois theorists. Their standpoint does not appear to him as merely illusory. On the contrary, the word 'crowd' (in the sense of *foule hétérogène*) rises from the past of Le Bon and Tarde to touch the present, as a precise portrait of the petty bourgeoisie. 'The mass as an impenetrable, compact entity [ . . . ] the subject of [ . . . ] "mass psychology" is [ . . . ] the petty bourgeoisie': not an imaginary phenomenon existing only in the mind of psychologists, criminologists or doctors versed in sociology but the product of a historical necessity, like 'mass psychology' itself. Thus,

78 Walter Benjamin, 'On the Concept of History' in *Selected Writings, Volume 4, 1938–1940* (Howard Eiland and Michael W. Jennings eds) (Cambridge, MA: Harvard University Press, 2003), p. 394.

Benjamin does not see in the crowd the character of an epoch (Le Bon's *l'ère de foules*) nor an anthropological constant but the expression of social tensions that have reached a certain degree of intensity. The crowd induces fear but it also appears in fear. One has only to recall the Marxist dictum: it is 'from its dream of itself' that the world must be awakened. Thus, the crowd that Le Bon called *foule homogène*—united by the same interests, educated in the same customs—must make way for the crowd that puts an end to all crowds. 'The struggling, oppressed class itself' emerges from the crowd in a kind of 'self-clarification' (*Selbstverständigung*).

**20.** 'What began in relation to the father is completed in relation to the mass.' Thus writes Freud in *Das Unbehagen in der Kultur* (*Civilization and Its Discontents*, 1929).[79] Opening *Massenpsychologie und Ich-analyse*, he wrote that the 'contrast between Individual and Social or Mass psychology, which at first glance may seem to be full of significance, loses a great deal of its sharpness when it is examined more closely'.[80] Benjamin rejects the epochal meaning of the concept of crowd, delimiting it and making it 'completely unusable for the purposes of fascism'; with what is in some respects a similar gesture, Freud instead refuses the idea that the social instinct and the herd instinct, the basic notions of crowd theory, are

79 Sigmund Freud, *Civilization and Its Discontents* in *The Complete Psychological Works of Sigmund Freud, Volume 21, 1927–1931* (James Strachey ed., in collaboration with Anna Freud, assisted by Alix Strachey and Alan Tyson) (New York: Vintage, 2001), p. 133. Translation modified (where the Standard Edition renders *Masse* as 'group').

80 Sigmund Freud, *Group Psychology and the Analysis of the Ego* (James Strachey trans.) (London: Hogarth Press and Institute of Psycho-Analysis, 1949), p. 1 (translation modified).

original and cannot be further broken down. For this very reason, however, he leads mass psychology back to individual psychology which, inseparable from the dynamic of family relations, appears in his eyes 'from the very first [as] Social Psychology'.[81] Le Bon's 'suggestion' and Tarde's 'imitation', as well as the magical power of 'prestige', are supplanted by the split between the Ego and moral conscience (a level internal to the Ego, the Ego ideal) and—*dis que c'est Œdipe, sinon t'auras une gifle!* ('Say it's Oedipus or else you'll get a slap in the face')[82]—by the identification with the father as the primary form of emotional bond, in other words, by the theory of goal-inhibited libidinal drives, which allows Freud to pass from the description of the crowd to that of durable and organized artificial masses. But this is already well known. One of the most radical aspects of Freud's essay is in fact that just as animosity and envy can be made out behind the relation of identification as the 'uncanny and coercive characteristics of group formations',[83] the most disturbing aspect of the horde can be made out behind the more stable social organization. Of course, we cannot but think of the essay's date of publication, of the war and the end of the hedonistic interpretation of the drives, of *Beyond the Pleasure Principle*. In other words, we cannot but be reminded of [Michel] Foucault's words (from *Maladie mentale et personnalité*, 1954; revised as *Maladie mentale et psychologie*, 1962):

> The social relations that determine a culture, in
> the form of competition, exploitation, group

81 Freud, *Group Psychology*, p. 2.

82 Gilles Deleuze and Félix Guattari, *Anti-Oedipus: Capitalism and Schizophrenia* (Robert Hurley, Mark Seem and Helen R. Lane trans) (Minneapolis: University of Minnesota Press, 1983), p. 45.

83 Freud, *Group Psychology*, p. 99.

rivalry, or class struggle, offer man an experience of his human environment that is permanently haunted by contradiction. [ . . . ] It is no accident that Freud, reflecting on the neuroses of war, should have discovered, as a counterweight for the life instinct, in which the old European optimism of the eighteenth century was still expressed, a death instinct, which introduced into psychology for the first time the power of the negative. Freud wished to explain war; but it was war that was dreamed in this shift in Freud's thinking.[84]

At the end of this already very Marxian passage from Foucault, we recognize again the phrase from Marx's letter to Ruge. With a proviso: in the 1921 essay, in which—as Paul Roazen has pointed out[85]—Freud retains his classical liberal model, it is the social *dispositif* founded on relations of exploitation, on the rivalry and antagonism that dreams itself as mass identification and the survival of the primal horde. Erich Fromm had already criticized as mere 'analogy' (*Analogie*) or 'similarity' (*Ähnlichkeit*) Freud's solution to the relationship between the individual and the collective, between the natural and the social. And yet, in referring social form back to the economy of drives, Freud also reveals that the economy of drives is a social economy; he shows that the tangle of familial ambivalences extends into the crowd at the very moment when the Church, the army and the horde penetrate the intimacy of libidinal relationships. War and capitalist society dream themselves in psychoanalysis;

84 Michel Foucault, *Mental Illness and Psychology* (Alan Sheridan trans.) (Berkeley: University of California Press, 1987), pp. 82–3.

85 Paul Roazen, *Freud: Political and Social Thought* (New York: Alfred A. Knopf, 1968).

but man can be awoken also and precisely because—to echo the fine title of an article by Otto Rank—psychoanalysis is 'a dream that interprets itself'.[86]

**21.** Another meditation that takes its cue from Lukács is Adorno's 1942 text 'Reflexionen zur Klassentheorie' ('Reflections on Class Theory'). Writing to Benjamin six years earlier, regarding the latter's essay on technical reproducibility, Adorno had set his hopes on a complete liquidation of the Brechtian themes in his friend's philosophy, pointing to 'the real consciousness of real proletarians, who in fact enjoy no advantage over their bourgeois counterparts apart from their interest in the revolution, and otherwise bear all the marks of mutilation of the typical bourgeois character'.[87] We might ask whether this observation is not in turn linked to the appearance (that is, to the false hypostasis) of a 'real consciousness', no matter how inefficient, maimed or gentrified it reveals itself to be. But in the conclusion of the 1942 essay—in one of the passages wherein he underscores his difference from Benjamin most forcefully—Adorno does explain himself quite clearly, illustrating what today we could call a process of subjectivation: 'The task of influencing people who beg to differ cannot be entrusted to films that stretch the credulity even of the like-minded. . . . Dehumanization is no external power, no propaganda.' Instead it is immanent to the system of the oppressed 'who used formerly to stand out because

86 Otto Rank, 'Ein Traum, der sich selbst deutet', *Jahrbuch für psychoanalytische und psychopathologische Forschungen* 2 (1910): 465–540.

87 Theodor W. Adorno and Walter Benjamin, *The Complete Correspondence, 1928–1940* (Henri Lonitz ed., Nicholas Walker trans.) (Cambridge: Polity, 1999), p. 131 (translation modified).

of their wretchedness, whereas today their wretchedness lies in the fact that they can never escape'.[88]

But exactly at this point, where proletarians have no real consciousness, where mass and proletariat, oppressors and oppressed blur into one another, the Adornian dialectic *dispositif* comes into play:

> This means, however, that the dehumanization is also its opposite. In reified human beings reification finds its outer limits. They catch up with the technical forces of production in which the relations of production lie hidden: in this way these relations lose the shock of their alien nature because the alienation is so complete. But they may soon also lose their power. Only when the victims completely assume the features of the ruling civilization will they be capable of wresting them from the dominant power. The only remaining differentiating factor is reduced to a naked usurpation. Only in its blind anonymity could the economy appear as fate: its spell is broken by the horror of the seeing dictatorship. The mimicking of the classless society by class society has been so successful that, while the oppressed have all been co-opted, the futility of all oppression becomes manifest. Even if the dynamic at work was always the same, its end today is not the end.[89]

Every page by Adorno is to be reread starting from the famous text with which *Minima Moralia* (1951)

88 Theodor W. Adorno, 'Reflections on Class Theory' in *Can One Live After Auschwitz? A Philosophical Reader* (Rolf Tiedemann trans., Rodney Livingstone et al. trans) (Stanford: Stanford University Press, 2003), pp. 109–10.

89 Ibid., p. 110.

concludes, but, at the same time, that aphorism is to be read starting from every page by Adorno: 'Perspectives must be fashioned that displace and estrange the world, reveal it to be, with its rifts and crevices, as indigent and distorted as it will appear one day in the messianic light.'[90] In terms of the 1942 'Reflections', this means first of all that it is necessary to avoid believing—as Brecht perhaps did—in the effective presence of class consciousness, showing instead this very category in a destructive light, in the poverty and inconsistency of its real precipitate. For Adorno, this is 'the simplest of all things, because the situation calls imperatively for such knowledge, indeed because consummate negativity, once squarely faced, delineates the mirror-image of its opposite'.[91] The conclusion of the 1942 text on class presents just such an inversion: if, according to the letter to Benjamin of 18 March 1936, 'The goal of the revolution is the elimination of fear',[92] now, when 'relations of production [ . . . ] lose the shock of their alien nature',[93] this seems to become the 'simplest of all things'. 'But'—and *Minima Moralia* are indeed a series of 'buts'—'it is also the utterly impossible thing, because it presupposes a standpoint removed, even though by a hair's breadth, from the scope of existence.'[94]

In its concluding passages, the 1942 essay seems to come up against this radical impossibility: it is only from a minimally exterior and already redeemed standpoint

90 Theodor W. Adorno, *Minima Moralia: Reflections on a Damaged Life* (E. F. N. Jephcott trans.) (London: Verso, 2005), p. 247.

91 Ibid.

92 Adorno and Benjamin, *The Complete Correspondence*, p. 131.

93 Adorno, 'Reflections on Class Theory', p. 110.

94 Adorno, *Minima Moralia*, p. 247.

that the terror of estrangement would be dispelled. Perhaps what comes to light in those final sentences is only the philosopher's position, his author-function as dictated by the relations of production themselves, a function at once protected by and expelled from the existent. Maybe it is thinking as such that finds itself always and already saved. Now, *Minima Moralia* declares: 'Even its own impossibility it must at last comprehend for the sake of the possible.'[95] Only here do the two texts really communicate: only for the philosopher who understands how the same impossibility in which he finds himself is defined by the circle of his 'bare usurpation' (still a magic circle, in its own way) do the words written in 1942 not presuppose an external point of view.

It was not Adorno but Benjamin who coined the most sober and rigorous formula for this kind of understanding. On 6 May 1934, Benjamin wrote to Gershom Scholem:

> [A]mong all the possible forms and means of expression, a credo is the last thing my communism resorts to [ . . . ] even at the cost of its orthodoxy—my communism is absolutely nothing other than the expression of certain experiences I have undergone in my thinking and in my life [ . . . ] it is a drastic, not infertile expression of the fact that the present intellectual industry finds it impossible to make room for my thinking, just as the present economic order finds it impossible to accommodate my life [ . . . communism] represents the obvious, reasoned attempt on the part of a man who is completely or almost completely deprived of any

---

95 Ibid.

means of production to proclaim his right to them, both in his thinking and in his life.[96]

A communism or love for the possible that is expressed here in its pure formula, that of an acknowledgement.

22. It goes without saying then that the philosopher cannot be a trailblazer who wraps himself in authoritativeness. A worthwhile philosophical task would instead be to study those phenomena in which what Le Bon called 'prestige' continues to exercise its influence on preformed masses (for instance in the cultural market, which administers the petty-bourgeois panic of not knowing, even furnishing that class with the ridiculous figure of the 'most influential philosopher').

In the cohesive crowd (or stock) to which Heidegger and Schmitt were glad to belong, the guide, the Führer, is (whether according to crowd theory or for other reasons) indistinguishable from his followers, but that is precisely why he has a following. 'Prestige' is an empty category but all the more active for it; within it, we also find the common and apparently opposing phenomena of the grotesque or 'Ubuesque' leader, to which Foucault drew attention, and of the guide who is ultimately nothing but a puppet. In the language of his time, Hippolyte Bernheim had advanced a precise diagnostic profile of this figure:

> Who has not seen those disinherited beings, who, not deprived of intelligence, are capable of assimilating current ideas, and even able to

96 Walter Benjamin and Gershom Scholem, *The Correspondence of Walter Benjamin and Gershom Scholem, 1932–1940* (Gershom Scholem ed., Gary Smith and Andre Lefevere trans) (Cambridge, MA: Harvard University Press, 1992), p. 110.

shine in their parlor, exhibiting illustrations of
their worth [ . . . ] but who are in reality wholly
without initiative and will power, without moral
resistance, and are carried along with the wind,
that is, wherever suggestion blows them? I
freely affirm that they are affected with instinctive imbecility.[97]

Tarde's pre-social being is the complementary opposite to the timid—what we have here is a subject, who,
so to speak, cannot but be part of a social circle. The animated mask is easy to recognize: it reminds us less of
the gloomy Marius Ratti[98] than of the fool Wenzel,[99] the
charismatic clown, the Weberian nightmare of our times.
Extremely easy to influence, irritable, quick to panic, the
little petty-bourgeois leader will rightly believe that thinking is not the precondition of acting, in this too following
a certain inspiration (*Suddenly I viddied that thinking
was for the gloopy ones and that the oomny ones used like
inspiration*); so, in the midst of suggestion, he will clearly
grasp what every leader imagines he knows: *Sheep,
thought I. But a real leader knows always, when like to give
and show generous to his unders.*[100] For he has to stick close
to his suggestible mass: he must first assure its compression the better to channel its explosions; paradoxically,
he must join it in order to be able to drag it behind him
or keep it at a distance, and let himself be admired. This
figure of leadership is thus the farthest removed from the
revolutionary guide imagined by Benjamin.

---

97 Hippolyte Bernheim, *Suggestive Therapeutics: A Treatise on the
Nature and Uses of Hypnotism* (Christian A. Herter trans.) (New
York and London: G. P. Putnam's Sons, 1880), p. 179.

98 [The protagonist of Hermann Broch's novel *The Spell*.]

99 [Ratti's henchman in *The Spell*.]

100 [Quotes in italics from Anthony Burgess' *A Clockwork Orange*.]

We cannot forget this: the 'mass' can be compressed—Joseph Dejacque defined government, in all its forms, as a *machine à compression*[101]—or slackened because

> it is not a thing with rigid properties but a process. That is because a multiplicity of individuals becomes a 'mass' in the specific sense only in certain known conditions and as long as these obtain. Being a mass is not equivalent to a sum of individuals [ . . . ] 'mass' is a process that happens in a more or less transitory way, differentiated according to degrees of intensity; it is quite changeable and fluctuating, as quick to disappear as it appeared, and it can arise in every human setting.[102]

The petty bourgeoisie is but the most favourable condition for the latent mass, and the Führer is its prime expression: 'the one who orients a multitude of individuals towards himself [ . . . ] with harangues or similar means, is in that moment its Führer, the psychological Führer of a latent mass'.[103] No doubt, the crowd needs a leader but—as Emil Lederer underlined[104]—he is not really chosen, nor does he pass any kind of test. How can he appear? Here the German is precise: *er wirft sich zum Führer auf*—he 'sets himself up' as leader, unexpectedly becoming the pole in the process of crystallization. Freud had explained the ease of this rise with the need for a

---

101 Joseph Déjacque, *La Question révolutionnaire* (New York: Barclay, 1854).

102 Georg Stieler, *Person und Masse. Untersuchungen zur Grundlegung einer Massenpsychologie* (Leipzig: Meiner, 1929), p. 149.

103 Ibid., p. 151.

104 Emil Lederer, *State of the Masses: The Threat of the Classless Society* (New York: W. W. Norton, 1940).

leader and the need for a leader with the libidinal economy of the Id. According to Hermann Broch—who in his
long and unfinished work on the madness of the masses,
*Massenwahntheorie*, reprises Freud's critique of social psychology—the mass always finds itself, by definition, in a
state of pre-panic (*Vor-Panic*) and the more it demands a
leader, the more it inexorably slides towards 'complete
panic' (*Voll-Panic*); it will thus not be a mythic 'non-
existent collective soul' (*nicht-existente Massenseele*) that
will orient all its anxieties, ecstatically transmuting them
into active hate for the stranger, but, rather, a concrete
person, a leader or a concrete group of functionaries.
Hannah Arendt's formula suits the latter well: the 'leader
is nothing more nor less than the functionary of the
masses he leads'.[105] Not a bureaucrat but one who, following his instinct, cannot but follow a directive. He
thus rises above the crowd with a singular fervour, never
ceasing to execute, as Broch said, his 'orienting function'
(*Ausrichtungsfunktion*).

Adorno relied on Freudian theory to ground his 'critical typology' in *The Authoritarian Personality*, whose
experimental apparatus, the famous 'F-scale', was in turn
elaborated on the basis of the psychoanalytic method of
free association. The conclusions are well known: *the
potentially fascist character exists*, which—'as a product
of interaction between the cultural climate of prejudice
and the "psychological" responses to this climate'[106]—
constitutes a single 'structural unity', albeit with a spectrum of dynamic and variegated manifestations. The

105 Hannah Arendt, *The Origins of Totalitarianism* (New York:
Harcourt Brace, 1973[1951]), p. 325.

106 Theodor W. Adorno, 'Types and Syndromes' in Theodor W.
Adorno, Else Frenkel-Brunswik, Daniel J. Levinson and R. Nevitt
Sanford, *The Authoritarian Personality* (New York: Harper & Brothers,
1950), p. 752.

'conventional' type is thus inseparable from the 'author-itarian submissive', as the latter is from the 'aggressive' or the 'manipulative' type whose 'lust for organization [ . . . ] seems boundless' and whose political concepts, Adorno pointedly underscores, 'are defined by the friend–foe relation, in exactly the same way as the Nazi theoretician Karl [sic] Schmitt defined the nature of pol-itics'.[107] It is exactly along this line of dynamic variation that the phenomenon is to be understood, according to a complex structure to which both the leader and the need for the leader belong. His rise to the status of leader corresponds to a certain degree of intensity within the same spectrum to which belongs the apparently more 'domestic' demeanour of the 'conventional' type. The Führer (or the celebrity, or the great man of prestige) is in fact a psychological subject just like, or indeed more than, his acolytes. As Freud specifies: 'He need only pos-sess the typical qualities of the individuals concerned in a particularly clearly marked and pure form.'[108] For their part, Joseph Delboeuf and Bernheim agreed that hypno-sis does not take the form of a vertical relationship, the direct domination by a waking subject who controls the sleep of another, but there are instead biunivocal, com-plex and collaborative currents; everywhere we only find 'different degrees and modes of suggestion'. Today, a Foucauldian might say that there are no subjects but only processes of suggestion. Already in 1913, Raoul Brugeilles pointed out (in an article later consulted by Freud) that in hypnosis there is more than just a play of strong impressions, of the most powerful subjectivities; there is a mass of suggestions, sometimes of minimal intensity, emanated by all individuals, often unawares.[109]

107 Ibid., p. 769.

108 Freud, *Group Psychology*, p. 102.

109 Raoul Brugeilles, 'L'Essence du phénomène social: la sugge-stion', *Revue de la France et de l'Étranger* 80 (1913): 593–602.

Regarding this question, theories themselves often imitate one another. And if 'even Bismarck and other very prominent party leaders [ . . . ] have emphasized the fact that inasmuch as they are leaders of a group, they are bound to follow it', if 'as a matter of fact, the leader allows himself to be led',[110] this has to do with the fact that his ego is—just like the other little egos compacted into the crowd—the latest product of reification. And because this petty-bourgeois ego is not subjected to a relationship of pure subjection, the subject still considers it a precious good to safeguard, in whose guise, if needs be, the social relation of commodification finds a way to cloak itself. Thus, though solidarity can survive amid the most brutal exploitation, in the petty-bourgeois panic only prestige proliferates. With its fluctuating valuations, prestige is the interest that accumulates and draws one towards the ego-commodity (and not so much towards the mere biological individual, which the ego-commodity survives or succumbs to).

The petty bourgeoisie is not, as Benjamin teaches us, a class: it is only a compressed mass between the rich bourgeoisie and the proletariat. From this non-class, every fascism will produce its 'people', masking this mere compression in the archaic and inseparable names of community, fatherland, work, blood, leader. The crowd, which according to Le Bon acquires a distorted but, in its own way, full consciousness in the prestigious leader, was ultimately nothing but a latent mass of leaders, still unwitting but ready to emerge. The consciousness of the revolutionary class is instead a limit-condition. Here every leader loses himself in the mass and it is even doubtful, according to Benjamin, whether one should

---

110 Georg Simmel, 'Fashion', *International Quarterly* 10 (1904): 141.

still employ the word 'consciousness'—a word that, after all, can also be applied to the commodity.

**23.** The old tycoon Harlan Potter does not tolerate intrusions into his family affairs. So, he summons Philip Marlowe to warn him, in the form of a moralizing sermon. Potter is a very rich and therefore very wise man: 'There's a peculiar thing about money,' he declares. 'In large quantities, it tends to have a life of its own, even a conscience of its own. The power of money becomes very difficult to control.'[111]

Money's conscience, its consciousness, is called interest. Interest is the self-reflection that money becomes capable of when it attains the greatest accumulations; it is the autonomous life of money that reproduces itself from money. And this life, albeit fleeting, is a power that does not allow itself to be dominated—if it is true that 'Interest, signifying the price of capital, is from the outset quite an irrational expression.'[112] These are the words of Marx, who explained the difference between new interest as a product in its own right, characteristic of capital, and the old usury. In his 1955 *Esquisse d'une psychologie des classes sociales*, Maurice Halbwachs reprised after his own fashion the famous pages of *Capital*, writing that

> The moneylender's trade was [ . . . ] a trade like any other, the profits limited by the laws against usury; and in fact it was followed only by those who had no other. The innovation that characterizes the capitalist system is the loan to

111 Raymond Chandler, *The Long Good-Bye* (London: Penguin, 2010[1953]), p. 275.

112 Karl Marx, *Capital, Volume 3* in Karl Marx and Friedrich Engels, *Collected Works*, VOL. 37 (London: Lawrence & Wishart, 1998), p. 352.

production, the advance to finance a productive undertaking. The moment this happens people start seeking in money the capacity to make more money. And once such a desire is conceived it can only increase indefinitely. Indeed, it is hard to see where its limits could lie. Money that is wanted for the consumer goods its procures disappears into the goods, in their consumption. [ . . . ] But money that is put out to make more money does not, in the first place, disappear, but increases. [ . . . ] Once money has acquired this capacity, it becomes its prime characteristic. Henceforth everything is valued in terms of money, goods, services, even time itself. [ . . . ] As [Benjamin] Franklin said: 'Remember, that time is money. He that can earn ten shillings a day by his labour, and goes abroad, or sits idly one half of that day, though he spends but sixpence during that diversion or idleness, ought not to reckon that the only expense; he has really spent, or rather thrown away, five shillings besides.' [ . . . ] To grow richer, not to have more goods, which will be consumed, but to have the means of becoming even richer: this is the new creed, a categorical imperative underlying capitalist morality.[113]

The biunivocal motto 'time is money' names interest and is the moral cipher inscribed in bourgeois consciousness.

---

113 Maurice Halbwachs, *The Psychology of Social Class* (Claire Delavenay trans., Georges Friedmann introd.) (Glencoe, IL: The Free Press, 1958), pp. 45–6.

It is precisely in the form: capital-interest that all intermediate links are eliminated, and capital is reduced to its most general formula, which therefore in itself is also inexplicable and absurd. The vulgar economist prefers the formula capital-interest, with its occult quality of making a value unequal to itself, to the formula capital-profit, precisely for the reason that this already more nearly approaches actual capitalist relations.[114]

Explaining how it is in the very nature of money to grow, Halbwachs still leaves this nature unexplained. Marx instead unveils the arcanum, expunging the myth of pure use in the form of money as equivalent of all commodities and incarnation of all social labour. Here too 'The hoarding drive is boundless in its nature'.[115] But there is nothing incomprehensible about this; instead it goes back to a basic contradiction. As we read in a famous passage from the first volume of *Capital*:

Qualitatively or formally considered, money is independent of all limits [*schrankenlos*], that is, it is the universal representative of material wealth because it is directly convertible into any other commodity. But at the same time every actual sum of money is limited in amount, and therefore has only a limited efficacy as a means of purchase. This contradiction between the quantitative limitation [*quantitative Schranke*] and the qualitative lack of limitation of money [*qualitative Schrankenlosigkeit*] keeps driving the

---

114 Marx, *Capital, Volume 3*, pp. 804–5.

115 Karl Marx, *Capital, Volume 1* (Ben Fowkes trans., Ernest Mandel introd.) (London: Penguin, 1976), p. 230.

hoarder back to his Sisyphean task: accumulation. He is in the same situation as a world conqueror, who discovers a new boundary with each
country he annexes.[116]

Time is money because this Sisyphean labour is a
fight against time. And since this undertaking without
pause or end is the only formula inscribed in every commodity, we are all hoarders, even acting as such when we
try to achieve the indispensable minimum. Because time
is money, anyone who wants to remain satisfied with his
six shillings of peace must work all the time. This is why
there is a capitalist ethic, and it does not stop existing
when its 'categorical imperative' only appears as a
solemn mask, threadbare and vain: whether cynical or
resigned, the disenchantment we now exhibit continues
to hide that time is in fact not money, that work is always
Sisyphean labour and, ultimately, 'absolute poverty'. To
grasp time's limit, transforming the unlimited into the
limited, the quantitative into the qualitative—this is
Marx's teaching. Materialism is therefore a philosophy
of history.

24. 'There was a man of the Island of Hawaii, whom I
shall call Keawe; for the truth is, he still lives, and his
name must be kept secret.' Keawe saw a nice house and
inside it a sad man looking at him. In fact, each envied
the other. The man showed Keawe his house and his
rooms.

> 'Truly,' said Keawe, 'this is a beautiful house; if
> I lived in the like of it, I should be laughing all
> day long. How comes it, then, that you should
> be sighing?' 'There is no reason,' said the man,
> 'why you should not have a house in all points

similar to this, and finer, if you wish. You have some money, I suppose?'[117]

The story is Robert Louis Stevenson's *The Bottle Imp* (1891), the tale of a magic object that guarantees every wish but which must be sold before one dies and always at a price lower than what was paid for it; the man who does not get rid of it in time—and there will be one who has bought the bottle at a minimal price below which it is impossible to go—will burn in hellfire. It will be the turn of the old, drunken boatswain, and the devil will come to collect the lien.

In this fable, interest's mysterious and cruel shadow, the semblance that profit cloaks itself in—namely, money's unlimited and spectral power—is captured, that is to say, critically elevated and restored to its rightful place. That place is a linguistic one. As in Stevenson, the power myth falls prey to the material power of language, which arises from need and exists only in relationships with other men. For this reason, interest is but an imp in the bottle. And the contradiction between individual and collective takes on a new meaning through the thick glass—that is, the material of fabulation—whereof the bewitched object is made. Individual life is limited. The contradiction between the quantitative and the qualitative tenor of money now presents itself as a contradiction between the unlimited time of individual life and the social aspect of the commodity-form. Life remains limited and the bottle—passing from hand to hand or from individual to individual—can offer everything except eternity. Even its power comes up against time and

117 Robert Louis Stevenson, 'The Bottle Imp' in *The Complete Stories of Robert Louis Stevenson* (Barry Menikoff ed.) (New York: Modern Library, 2002), p. 577.

is therefore, like the power of money, qualitatively unlimited and quantitatively limited.

Between the qualitatively unlimited and the quantitatively limited, there will always be an excess commodity which cannot be bought (or sold): the bottle, precisely. Whence the need for accumulation:

> 'I have fifty dollars,' said Keawe; 'but a house like this will cost more than fifty dollars.' The man made a computation. 'I am sorry you have no more,' said he, 'for it may raise you trouble in the future; but it shall be yours at fifty dollars.' 'The house?' asked Keawe. 'No, not the house,' replied the man; 'but the bottle.'[118]

Not the house (recall Pound: 'With usura hath no man a house of good stone'[119]), but the pure object of exchange, the universal equivalent that, with diabolical consciousness, money itself purchases and increases. The less you accumulate, the lower the interest in your favour; the less money you have, the lower the figure you can pay at present, the more easily 'it may raise you trouble in the future'; the higher and more threatening the price you have to pay, the nearer and more inevitable its collection. The lower the figure, the shorter the time, the higher the interest climbs. In the end, who becomes a slave to the devil? Who remains bound hands and feet? The poorest, the one who has far less than fifty dollars, the one who can buy the commodity only at the lowest price. The one whose chains are already tight. In the third volume of *Capital*, Marx explains more clearly than Halbwachs the difference between old and the new

118 Ibid., p. 578.

119 Ezra Pound, 'Canto XLV' in *The Cantos of Ezra Pound* (London: Faber and Faber, 1975), p. 229.

usury: if usury, which played a revolutionary function in pre-capitalist systems, destroying the old forms of property (in effect: 'with usury / seeth no man Gonzaga his heirs and his concubines')[120]

> not content with squeezing the surplus labour out of his victim, gradually acquires possession even of his very conditions of labour, land, house, etc., and is continually engaged in thus expropriating him [ . . . ] this complete expropriation of the labourer from his conditions of labour is not a result which the capitalist mode of production seeks to achieve, but rather the established prerequisite for its point of departure. The wage slave, just like the real slave, cannot become a creditor's slave due to his position—at least in his capacity as producer; the wage slave, it is true, can become a creditor's slave in his capacity as consumer.[121]

What is interest? The answer lies in the question: What is profit? Which in turn brings us to another: Who becomes the slave of interest? The one who can *only* buy the bottle, who, already a slave in his capacity as a producer, can only become a slave as a consumer. He—the old drunkard, boatswain, deserter, miner and felon—buys the bottle because he cannot even fear hell any longer: 'I reckon I'm going anyway . . . and this bottle's the best thing to go with I've struck yet.'[122]

**25.** His figure is the last one taken by the real (i.e. psychological) consciousness of the poor little ego, that

---

120 Ibid.

121 Marx, *Capital, Volume 3*, p. 590.

122 Stevenson, 'The Bottle Imp', p. 604.

is of the slave who thinks (that he thinks). His last act is an act of desperate opportunism. For opportunism—whose link to warmongering was demonstrated by Rosa Luxemburg—is the vilest form of desperation. It remains attached to interest, namely, to particular interest, like the drunkard to the bottle. As Lukács noted: '[O]pportunism *mistakes the actual, psychological state of consciousness of proletarians for the class consciousness of the proletariat'.*[123] His path was that of reformist trade-unionism through which the petty-bourgeois mass was able to lodge itself into the proletariat and expand.

But the story of dissolutions sketched out by Marx in the *Grundrisse* has been supplemented by a stage that renders trade-unions themselves superfluous: it is that of the contemporary forms of work aimed at finding work, which are present, as a kind of meta-labour, in every kind of work and beyond all work. From this derive certain bizarre phenomena such as voluntary work, that is, work without salary in the hope of finding work. The classical role of the unemployed is now taken up by the worker and their figures are blurred. We are here in truly murky waters, in which now swims consciousness, which has the same entirely psychological character as meta-labour (or absolute surplus value). Only one thing remains true: '*Someone may castigate and flagellate himself all day long like the monks etc., and this quantity of sacrifice he contributes will remain totally worthless.* [ . . . ] There has to be something besides sacrifice.'[124]

123 Lukács, *History and Class Consciousness*, p. 74.

124 Karl Marx, *Grundrisse* (Martin Nicolaus trans.) (London: Penguin, 1973), p. 613.

**26.** How then are we to think about the class consciousness and revolutionary solidarity of which Benjamin speaks?

The reply may be found in one of Marx's most beautiful questions—which is really also the invention of a problem: *What is a working day?* And what is this 'ultima Thule' which is the necessary limit of the working day? Recall Marx's dialectical staging in a passage from the first volume of *Capital*, where we hear the voices—which had never rung as clearly—of the capitalist and the worker. The former

> takes his stand on the law of commodity-exchange. Like all other buyers, he seeks to extract the maximum possible benefit from the use-value of his commodity. Suddenly, however, there arises the voice of the worker, which had previously been stifled in the sound and fury of the production process: 'The commodity I have sold you differs from the ordinary crowd of commodities in that its use creates value, a greater value than it costs. That is why you bought it. [ . . . ] You are constantly preaching to me the gospel of "saving" and "abstinence". Very well! Like a sensible, thrifty owner of property I will husband my sole wealth, my labour-power, and abstain from wasting it foolishly. [ . . . ] I demand a normal working day because, like every other seller, I demand the value of my commodity'.[125]

The voice of the worker echoes the strike declaration of the London builders in 1860–61. Marx comments as follows:

125 Marx, *Capital, Volume 1*, pp. 342–3.

We see then that, leaving aside certain extremely elastic restrictions [*Schranken*], the nature of commodity exchange imposes no limit [*Grenze*] to the working day, no limit to surplus labour. The capitalist maintains his rights as a purchaser when he tries to make the working day as long as possible, and, where possible, to make two working days out of one. On the other hand, the peculiar nature of the commodity sold implies a limit to its consumption by the purchaser, and the worker maintains his right as a seller when he wishes to reduce the working day to a particular normal length.[126]

We can recognize here a further manifestation of the same schema that accounted for the mechanism of accumulation. There, the contradiction between limited and unlimited gave rise to the infinite task, the Sisyphean labour of the conqueror of money. Here there is a similar contrast, between a tendentially unlimited surplus value and the limit to its consumption by the capitalist purchaser. This contradiction reproduces at another level that between the quantitative limit and the qualitative limitlessness of money, giving rise to another infinite undertaking, the Sisyphean labour of the contractual negotiation between worker and capitalist.

Nevertheless, in that passage from *Capital* something entirely different also rears its head, namely, a decisive 'antinomy' (*Antinomie*). This antinomy is not a clash between the limited and the unlimited. Instead, it is founded on the highly ironic notion of a *normal* working day—ironic because such a day could never exist under the very conditions in which it is demanded, in which its

126 Ibid., p. 344.

need arises. As is clearly stated, if there were no surplus value nobody would buy the labour-commodity and no voice of protest would be raised (as Marx says in another famous passage, if the whole working day were reduced to its *absolute minimum limit*, to its necessary but contractile constitutive component, 'surplus labour would vanish, something which is impossible under the regime of capital'[127]). In the conditions under which the voice makes itself heard, in the dominion of capital as boundless drive, a working day could never be *normal*; it will always be excessive, laden with surplus labour. Whence the irony resounding in the worker's voice: 'You preach abstinence to me? [ . . . ] well, I'll take you at your word.' In other words, my drive to save will be, and cannot but be, as unlimited as your drive to earn. Thus, the antinomy transpires *in each and every word*: not only a clash between differing and opposing voices but a contradiction inherent in the very law of exchange that cannot be resolved by any new contract (by any concealment of the antinomy amid the infinite flowerings of the pure contractual formula: 'You preach saving to me? Then I will work more').

Here the *nomos* of political economy folds back and turns upon itself: 'There is here therefore an antinomy, of right against right, both equally bearing the seal of the law of exchange. Between equal rights, force decides.'[128] It's at this point, when the din of the production process is halted, that a voice suddenly rises and class appears: 'Hence, in the history of capitalist production, the establishment of a norm for the working day [*Normierung des Arbeitstag*] presents itself as a struggle over the limits of that day, a struggle between collective

127 Ibid., p. 667.
128 Ibid., p. 344.

capital [*Gesamtkapitalist*], i.e. the class of capitalists, and collective labour [*Gesamtarbeiter*], i.e. the working class.'[129]

Here everything happens within the dynamic of the commodity and according to the laws of exchange, which unexpectedly interrupt their advance, reaching an antinomic situation. Here the labourer [*operaio*] or better the worker [*lavoratore*]—since the term *Arbeiter* precedes the 'division' (*Teilung*) between physical and intellectual activity—does not answer with the voice of psychological consciousness but in terms of the reduction of his own existence to a commodity. Reprising the topos of the *Science of Logic* so dear to Marx, Lukács will argue that for the worker the quantitative becomes qualitative; what the capitalist tries to pass off as a mere quantity of commodities reveals itself to the worker as pure quality, as his own existence. Yet this 'existence' appears charged with revolutionary possibilities only if at the same time—Marx here should be read to the letter—it is nothing more than a commodity, that is, money. In the real antinomy, what from one angle presents itself as unlimited—for there is nothing in the worker's day that cannot be converted into money—does not just clash with life as finite time and limited commodity, nor with the capitalist's limited capacity to have commodities at his disposal (with the limits of his life as an accumulator). There is indeed a limit in the labour-commodity that *really* requires parsimony or 'saving'. But the ironic tenor of this 'saving' goes beyond the simple contradiction between limited and unlimited, as well as the bad infinite of the contractual relation (with its desperate accounting: How many more parts of my limited life must I surrender to you so as to live what remains of my life?). The parsimonious worker knows very well that he can be bought at every instant,

129 Ibid.

*but exactly for this reason he also knows that there is no instant that cannot be saved*; unlike the bad trade-unionist, the worker *truly* uses the logic of exchange; he cleaves closely to the unlimited character of money. Here even the qualitatively unlimited power of money suddenly finds a similar power confronting it; the unlimited, so to speak, folds back on itself and really reaches an endpoint. *Only here does the antinomy arise because the unlimited encounters its end only in the other unlimited that stands opposed to it.*

Everything happens because the proletarian never for a moment stops being what he really is: object, commodity, money. His sight is never blocked and blurred by his own ego which, perhaps disguised as an object, laments its trampled rights; before him he only has an object: the mass of commodities or money which, without any separation, he also (and at the same time) is.

The worker here does not act and raise his voice merely to obtain a little free time (which will only benefit his antagonist, since the worker will only work better and consume more). But that time which is alien from work—the time of *paresse* and not *loisir*, as Lafargue taught—matters a lot to him.[130] This is because the worker acts totally to transform his life thanks precisely to the energies that life without work has deposited and nurtured in him. It is the energies of love that now, in the brutal reduction to the status of object, come to his rescue. For in love, as Marx explains in *The Holy Family* (1845), there is nothing subjective and it is love 'which first really teaches man to believe in the objective world

---

130 Paul Lafargue, *Le Droit à la paresse (Réfutation du «Droit au travail» de 1848)* (Paris: Maspero, 1969[1883]).

outside himself, which not only makes man into an object, but even the object into a man!'[131]

27. When the antinomy comes to light, the productive process comes to a halt and the antagonism between worker and capitalist becomes *ipso facto* class struggle. Perhaps only at this level can one talk of 'class consciousness'. And if the word 'consciousness' has a meaning here—which only appears paradoxical at first sight—it is that of the simple attainment, within the revolutionary class, of neutrality between the categories of subject and object.

This neutralization is called solidarity. To be conscious means to struggle, to be solidary or objects of solidarity. Solidarity is not the basis of the community that in turn, as in Edith Stein, comes before the state.[132] And solidarity is not a good intention of the ego, but the form of the simple existence of class, namely, as revolutionary class. Only the homespun conformist separates solidarity, a feeling so dear to him, from struggle, which he instead despises more than anything (while the sophisticated conformist will laugh at this detached solidarity, the only one that he knows). For the conscious revolutionary class, struggle and solidarity are instead indissoluble, they communicate with one other intimately.

Benjamin describes class struggle as a loosening or distension. And the mass as a compression. But it is exactly in this mass—which is no longer 'an abstract,

131 Karl Marx and Friedrich Engels, *The Holy Family, or Critique of Critical Criticism: Against Bruno Bauer and Company* in *Collected Works, Volume 4* (London: Lawrence & Wishart, 1975), pp. 21–2.

132 Edith Stein, *An Investigation Concerning the State* (Marianne Sawicki trans.) (Washington, DC: ICS Publications, 2006).

immutable "mass"'[133]—that loosenings can arise. When Benjamin writes that in the petty bourgeoisie there is a non-dialectical contradiction between the individual and the mass, he seems to follow not only Marx but also Lukács. In fact, he seems almost indistinguishable from the latter: the individual and class consciousness are also for Benjamin (as with the peasant petty bourgeoisie) in a relationship of 'contradictory [*kontradiktorisch*] opposition' that is not yet dialectical.

But Lukács reprises and transforms a passage on social democracy from *The Eighteenth Brumaire*, writing:

[T]he petty bourgeoisie [ . . . ] is directly exposed to the influence of capitalism [ . . . ] it cannot possibly remain wholly unaffected by the *fact* of class conflict between bourgeoisie and proletariat. But as a 'transitional class in which the interests of two other classes become simultaneously blunted . . . ' it will imagine itself 'to be above all class antagonisms'. Accordingly it will search for ways whereby it will 'not indeed eliminate the two extremes of capital and wage labour, but will weaken their antagonism and transform it into harmony'.[134]

We could note that while Lukács quotes Marx, he does not completely follow him. It is true that Marx is describing 'a democratic transformation of society within the frame of the petty bourgeoisie', but he is not exactly providing a description of this scenario.

We cannot fail to note that here Benjamin completely inverts Lukács. In the scenario that confronts him,

---

133 Marx and Engels, *The Holy Family*, p. 80.

134 Lukács, *History and Class Consciousness*, pp. 59–60. The passages quoted by Lukács are from Marx.

the petty bourgeoisie is still transitional and therefore compressed. With Weimar social democracy, this compression lasted enough to explode into Nazism. No doubt there were attenuations of the extremes but their effect (for example, in the alliance with the unemployed) was merely to add to the ranks of the petty bourgeoisie, which is through and through a dangerous crowd. The words which the reactionary Le Bon used to describe both revolutionary and criminal fit it all too well, and find in the reactions of the petty-bourgeois crowd their moment of truth.

**28.** Marx had already written in *The Poverty of Philosophy* that 'Large-scale industry concentrates in one place [*endroit*] a crowd of people unknown to one another. Competition divides their interests.'[135] Barely over a year earlier, in *The Condition of the Working Class in England* (1845), Engels had observed that 'the dissolution of mankind into monads' [*Auflösung der Menschheit in Monaden*], the isolation of each individual in his egoism, 'is nowhere so shamelessly barefaced, so self-conscious, as just here in the crowding [*Gewühl*] of the great city'.[136] Urbanization continues the same movement, it deploys and organizes outside the factory a crowd of people unknown to one another: it does not eliminate the crowd but offers it shelter; it dissimulates, distributes and maintains it as a latent phenomenon; it amplifies and dissolves it while readying the stage for its sudden crystallizations.

135 Marx, *The Poverty of Philosophy*, p. 210.
136 Friedrich Engels, *The Condition of the Working Class in England* in Karl Marx and Friedrich Engels, *Collected Works, Volume 4* (London: Lawrence & Wishart, 1975), p. 329.

Almost a century later, in 1925, Robert Ezra Park sees the metropolis as an unstable aggregate 'in a chronic condition of crisis'.[137] His paradigm is exactly the crowd, which Park had studied during his years in Germany, under the influence of Simmel and in the school of Windelband. But the expression 'psychological moment' employed by Park still designates a relative instability; it is revealed as a euphemism when crises are normal and tensions are such that 'a slight cause may precipitate an enormous effect'.[138] As the 'nerve centre of the social organism',[139] the city is instead shaken by rapid and intense fluctuations, like those of the Stock Exchange; the crowd vibrates and reacts with the same ease as the market and it can be controlled, Park observes, just like stock valuations are controlled and manipulated by speculators.

For, now quoting Benjamin's 1938 'The Paris of the Second Empire in Baudelaire':

> [T]he crowd really is a spectacle of nature—if one may apply this term to social conditions. A street, a conflagration, or a traffic accident assembles people who are not defined along class lines. They present themselves as concrete gatherings, but socially they remain abstract [ . . . ] Their models are the customers who, each acting in his private interest, gather at the market around their 'common cause'". In many

137 Robert E. Park, 'The City: Suggestions for the Investigation of Human Behavior in the Urban Environment' in Robert E. Park, Ernest W. Burgess and Roderick D. McKenzie, *The City: Suggestions for the Investigation of Human Behavior in the Urban Environment* (Chicago: The University of Chicago Press, 1967[1925]), p. 22.

138 Ibid., p. 20.

139 Ibid., p. 23.

cases, such gatherings have only a statistical existence. This existence conceals the really monstrous thing about them: that the concentration of private persons as such is an accident resulting from their private concerns. But if these concentrations become evident—and totalitarian states see to this by making the concentration of their citizens permanent and obligatory for all their purposes—their hybrid character is clearly manifest, particularly to those who are involved. They rationalize the accident of the market economy which brings them together in this way as 'fate' in which 'the race' is reunited. In doing so, they give free rein to both the herd instinct and to reflective action. The peoples who are in the foreground of the western European stage make the acquaintance of the supernatural which confronted Hugo in the crowd.[140]

140 Walter Benjamin, 'The Paris of the Second Empire in Baudelaire' in *Selected Writings, Volume 4, 1938–1940* (Howard Eiland and Michael W. Jennings eds) (Cambridge, MA: Belknap Press, 2003), pp. 36–7. A variant of this passage, as well as of the 1936 note, can be found in *Passagenwerk* J 81 a, 1: '[T]he mass as such has no primary social significance. [ . . . ] A theater audience, an army, the population of a city comprise masses which in themselves belong to no particular class. The free market multiplies these masses [*Massen*], rapidly and on a colossal scale, insofar as each merchandise now gathers around it the crowd [*Menge*] of its potential buyers. The totalitarian states have taken this mass as their model. The *Volksgemeinschaft* [People's Community] aims to root out from single individuals everything that stands in the way of their wholesale fusion into a mass of consumers. The one implacable adversary still confronting the state, which in this ravenous action becomes the agent of monopoly capital, is the revolutionary proletariat. This latter dispels the illusion of the mass through the

Paris, capital of the nineteenth century. The expression comes, of course, from the young Marx. But when Benjamin reprises it in the mid 1930s, he foregrounds the figure of the crowd which pushes up against his own present. Poetry, like Baudelaire's *flânerie*, becomes knowable for Benjamin only in the 'moment of danger' in which the organized fascist crowd pours onto the streets. As an illusory phenomenon, which feigns to possess the principle of its own movement within itself, to be endowed with its own soul, the great nineteenth-century crowd—which having left the fairs and boulevards breaks up and lingers in the *passages*—now appears as 'the empty mold with which, seventy years later, the *Volksgemeinschaft* [People's Community] was cast. The flâneur [ . . . ] was the first to fall victim to an ignis fatuus which since that time has blinded many millions'.[141]

This illusion, moreover, leads one to believe that the accidental, temporary and '*par excellence heterogeneous*' aggregate is *opposed to social homogeneity*. This appearance, concentrated in the figure of the leader, is still present in Georges Bataille's 'La structure psychologique du fascisme' (1933): 'Opposed to democratic politicians, who represent in different countries the platitude inherent to *homogeneous* society, Mussolini and Hitler immediately stand out as something *other*.'[142] According to Bataille, the fascist state would have reunited in itself two opposing elements, pure sovereignty and the apparatus. Here the old matrix reappears in the idea of a sovereign

reality of class' (Benjamin, *The Arcades Project*, pp. 370–1; translation modified).

141 Benjamin, *The Arcades Project*, pp. 345–6.

142 Georges Bataille, 'The Psychological Structure of Fascism' in *Visions of Excess: Selected Writings, 1927–1939* (Allan Stoekl ed.) (Minneapolis: University of Minnesota Press, 1985), p. 143.

heterogeneity. If, in Bataille, both the ranks and leaders in uniform and the wretched classes in revolt are '*totally other*' with regard to homogenous and productive normality, the negative spectre of the crowd—which had already reared its head in Tarde or Sighele—now makes itself manifest everywhere at the margins of society.

Not only does the revolutionary class not fit this schema, it nullifies it. In a first version of the note on class, which we've already cited, Benjamin in fact wrote: 'The formation of masses does not in any way happen only within classes' [*Die Formierung von Massen geht keineswegs allein im Schosse von Klassen vor sich*], but following an inverse movement, 'the formation of classes happens within masses' [*die Formierung der Klassen erfolge im Schosse von Massen*]. Therefore, the revolutionary class only follows the crowd in a temporal order, according to the 'concrete and reasonable' process through which it distinguishes and isolates itself from the crowd.[143]

Homogeneous society and heterogeneous crowd appear opposed and yet remain tied to each other. But the revolutionary class, which emerges and emancipates itself from the apparent community, from the crowd, overcomes this opposition too and dissolves every bond. There is no longer an orderly plain from which something 'suddenly arises'; if a haughty, sovereign aura envelops the leader, solidarity dissolves it.

**29.** *Was ist Aura?* The text that begins with these words was unpublished until recently.[144] Benjamin probably

---

143 Benjamin, *Gesammelte Schriften VII.2*, p. 668.

144 It is among the manuscripts found by Giorgio Agamben in the Bibliothèque Nationale of Paris in 1981. It can be read in the Walter Benjamin Archiv in Berlin. I thank Clemens-Carl Härle who

wrote it at the beginning of 1935 while he was preparing 'The Work of Art in the Age of Its Technological Reproducibility', even if nothing prevents us from envisaging a later elaboration, perhaps owing to Adorno's critical reception of the 'Work of Art' essay; in a kind of counterpoint to that famous text, the cinematographic instrument here appears in its typically reactionary function, adapted to the power relations instituted by capitalism.

In any case, the three small sheets, torn out from a bar pad embellished with the San Pellegrino red star and entirely covered in minute handwriting, contain a well-known definition that can also be found verbatim or with minimal variations both in the essay on technical reproducibility (already in the 1936 version) as well as in 'On Some Motifs in Baudelaire' (1939).

What is aura? 'The one who is seen or believes himself to be seen [glances up] answers with a gaze'. When this normal social reaction is transferred into the relationship between man and nature, then—writes Benjamin—the auratic experience takes place. Then, every animate or inanimate being gazes back at us. This is the experience of distance that belongs to the oneiric realm: '[I]ts glance is dreaming, draws us after its dream [*sein Blick traümt, zieht uns seinem Traume nach*] [ . . . ] As

---

allowed me to consult his careful transcription. The text is partially reproduced (with a reproduction of the original) in *Walter Benjamin's Archive: Images, Texts, Signs* (Ursula Marx, Gudrun Schwarz, Michael Schwarz and Erdmut Wisizla eds; Esther Leslie trans.) (London: Verso, 2007), p. 45. The first publication of Benjamin's note in full was in Agamben's Italian translation, as 'Che cos'è l'aura?' in Walter Benjamin, *Charles Baudelaire. Un poeta lirico nell'età del capitalismo avanzato* (Giorgio Agamben, Barbara Chitussi and Clemens-Carl Härle eds) (Vicenza: Neri Pozza Editore, 2012), pp. 25–6.

much aura in the world as there is still dream in it [*Soviel Aura in der Welt als nach Traum in ihr*].' Yet the three sheets also speak of the moment when the dream is extinguished and the aura fades while 'the awakened eye' [*das erwachte Auge*] does not lose its capacity to observe. The theory of perception turns here into a theory of class. Another gaze appears, one that has lost all distance and all magic and instead recalls the way in which the eyes of the despised meet those brimming with contempt; this is the nearest gaze, with which the oppressed answers the oppressor.

When the tension between the classes reaches a certain level [*Grad*], this gaze emerges in its mass form. As Benjamin writes: 'Here we come up against an antinomy' [*es kommt zu einer Antinomie*]. In such a situation, the classes would like to study one another and the dominators in particular would want to observe the dominated; but the latter are all the more able to shield themselves from their gazes with their own fierce and threatening ones. Then the exploiters do not dare to go any further, they even stop entering the workplace; and the conditions in which the majority of the exploited live become ever more obscure to them.

It is at this point that cinematographic technique enters the fray. It advantageously allows one to study others without being seen or studied oneself; it hides one from those gazes while concealing the dangers of social life. The camera (then as now, one might say) protects from class hatred. As the short text concludes: 'Without cinema, the decadence of the aura would become evident in an ultimately unbearable way' [*Ohne den Film würde man den Verfall der Aura in einem nicht mehr erträglichen Masse zu Spüren zu bekommen*].

'I have found that aspect of nineteenth-century art that is only knowable "now" [*der nur 'jetzt' erkennbar ist*], which never was before and never will be again,'[145] Benjamin wrote to Gretel Adorno on the 9 October 1935, announcing the essay 'The Work of Art in the Age of Its Technological Reproducibility'. But the moment of this knowledge, in which cinema also reveals its revolutionary aspect, is the same as the one spoken of in the fragment on aura. Both the oppressors and the oppressed would like to study each other. The former possess a new instrument and can examine the latter while remaining concealed. There is something, however, that resists their gazes, in spite of the camera. From outside, in the representations of their oppressors, 'the class-conscious proletariat' will appear only as 'a compact mass'. Hatred can be felt and studied but solidarity is one of its invisible degrees which cannot and must not be dissimulated and from which it is impossible to hide. By definition, it is invisible to those who are not in solidarity. Unseen by the oppressor, the class in solidarity will then be able to appropriate the camera, and from within the true antinomy—'from a *changed* foundation of production, a new foundation first created by the process of history'[146]—it will be able to cast an equally new gaze.

**30.** What of solidarity cannot be grasped from the outside? What renders it entirely unknowable?

In *The Poverty of Philosophy*, we read: 'Economic conditions had first transformed the mass of the people . . .

145 Gretel Adorno and Walter Benjamin, *Correspondence, 1930–1940* (Henri Lonitz and Christopher Gödde eds; Wieland Hoban trans.) (Cambridge: Polity, 2008), p. 166 (translation modified).

146 Marx, *Grundrisse*, p. 833.

into workers. The domination of capital has created for this mass a common situation, common interests. This mass is thus already a class as against capital, but not yet for itself'.[147] From the point of view of capital, it is precisely this class which is—in Benjamin's terms—a 'mass as such'; its common interests are still mere interests, that is, pre-formed by capital itself. As Marx writes: 'In the struggle . . . this mass becomes united, and constitutes itself as a class for itself'.[148] The authentic constitution of the class therefore does not happen before struggle, nor through it, but in the *medium* of struggle (*dans la lutte*). But this is not a mere clash. Marx identifies the essential aspect of workers' resistance: it does not aim at maintaining a wage but, rather, a 'combination'. With combination, which aims at 'stopping competition among the workers',[149] begins solidarity; what begins, we could say, is loosening, and something becomes invisible: 'This is so true that English economists are amazed to see the workers sacrifice a good part of their wages in favour of associations, which, in the eyes of these economists, are established solely in favour of wages'.[150]

For this reason, in the words of the *Manifesto*, '[t]he communists disdain to conceal their views and aims';[151] what their enemies could never recognize is the essential aspect of the antinomy. The formula 'there is no instant of work that cannot be saved' is in fact the least subjective; in it, all contradictions between individual and society dissolve. It does not concern small groups, nor does

---

147 Marx, *The Poverty of Philosophy*, p. 211.

148 Ibid.

149 Ibid., p. 210.

150 Ibid., p. 211.

151 Marx and Engels, *Manifesto of the Communist Party*, p. 519.

it say: 'there is no instant of mine . . . ' or 'an instant of a certain job . . . ' or 'there is no instant here and now (for us who are thus employed) . . . '. Instead, it touches the unlimited and affirms: there is no instant . . . where there is not a proletarian for whom there is no instant . . . where there is not a proletarian with whom one cannot be in solidarity. 'In short, the Communists everywhere support every revolutionary movement.'[152]

This struggle—in Jean Fallot's words, an *effective solidarity*, and not a fight for power'[153]—is then, according to the Marxist dictum, 'a veritable civil war'. It throws into disarray the antagonisms that regulate capitalist society, heralding the classless society. It is in solidarity that 'all the elements necessary for a coming battle unite and develop. Once it has reached this point, association takes on a political character'.[154]

What does this mean? Once again, Carl Schmitt comes to mind: for him civil war is the real and present possibility that politically constitutes the space of the state. For him, war, as the possibility of a 'clear' and 'concrete' distinction between friend and enemy, is the inner principle of every association. On the contrary, in Marx, the inner principle and presupposition of political struggle is solidarity, that is to say, association, and struggle thus means the destruction of the state.

(Fake) civil war is the rule of the crowd (which the state both placates and organizes). The 'veritable civil war' is the work of the class, which looks like a crowd only from the outside. For there is no outside to solidarity;

---

152 Ibid.

153 Jean Fallot (Antoine Brognard), *Lutte de classe et morale marxiste* (Aubenas: Lienhart et Cie, 1968), p. 231.

154 Marx, *The Poverty of Philosophy*, p. 211.

when it comes to solidarity, the outside does not even constitute a point of view.

31. '[I]f the danger doesn't come in the form of brigands, it is coming from somewhere else.'[155] The idea is trivial. But it enacts the transformation of the mass into a homicidal crowd, of the widespread fear of 1789 into a 'persecutory (aggressive) neurotic anxiety', preparing the affective identification with the *leader* and introducing the conspiracy theory of history. And if, according to Franz Neumann's famous thesis, the latter requires a false concreteness, 'at least a grain of truth',[156] the proposition *'if the danger does not come . . . it comes from elsewhere'* goes even deeper and says: *the truth is to be found in neurotic anxiety itself*, the real danger is everywhere because it always comes from elsewhere, it is constituted itself on the basis of its own absence.

If Neumann recognizes, at the bottom of every alarmist voice, a kernel of truth, however distorted it might be, it is because he has already accepted that fear is founded on danger. But *le péril vient d'ailleurs*, and so does panic. We can say that where there is a crowd, or even a mass on the way to becoming a crowd, *the elementary precondition of fear is not at all danger but the very reaction that fear engenders*. The apparent effect is the real cause.

'Is this dark crowd [*dumpfe Menge*] not perhaps waiting for a disaster, big enough to make it throw off the sparks of its accumulated tension, a conflagration or

155 Tarde, 'Conviction and the Crowd', p. 236.

156 Franz Neumann, *Behemoth: The Structure and Practice of National Socialism, 1933–1944* (Chicago, IL: Ivan R. Dee, 2009 [1944]), p. 469

maybe the end of the world, something capable of
turning this dampened murmur of a thousand voices
into a single scream [ . . . ] ?'[157] Prolonged shivers shake it,
innumerable ghosts do not stop conspiring, the great irritable body is jolted but there are no subtle strategies at
play. Terror does not demand them; it is animated instead
by a more elemental chemistry. A certain fear gradually
insinuates itself, which adds to the compression and
renders the fear even more acute and real. The exercise
of power will not be about capturing, transforming or
guiding actions—perhaps an impossible task—but about
making sure that not a single one of them is carried out,
pre-emptively provoking the widest range of reactions.
This is because inertia and revenge imply each other.
Superficially excitable, unable to act, the compressed
masses waver and abandon themselves to a deeper
stupefaction.

**32.** Though the crowd was a typical subject matter of
nineteenth-century realism, Goya captured it in the
whites of the eyes of the pilgrims of San Isidro: gazes sat-
urated with what Mario Praz called 'hopeless stupor',[158]
terrifying stares on faces that cannot be awakened. This
vacuity will be disclosed once again, ultimately spreading
over the entire expanse of Paris. [Eugene] Atget's city is
not in fact deserted, it is the city of the looming crowd
that no one seems able to avoid; it is the city of the crowd

157 Walter Benjamin, 'Schönes Entsetzen' (1929) in *Gesammelte
Schriften IV.1* (Tillman Rexroth ed.) (Frankfurt: Suhrkamp, 1991),
p. 434.
158 Mario Praz, *Mnemosyne: The Parallel between Literature and the
Visual Arts* (Princeton, NJ: Princeton University Press, 1970), p.
176.

that collectively dreams it and can thus no longer glimpse the presence of anyone.

It is worth repeating that this slow visionary torpor is also and perhaps mostly at work in moments of great excitement. It is a sleep that does not just come over you when everything is calm; it was there before, even in great bygone revolts, in those salient instants when the drums beat and cries were raised.

This sleep later became the dream of cinema. It must be noted again that the cinematographic instrument can be of comfort to the powers that be, it is because it confirms and reproduces the exteriority of the point of view. That is why class can only appear as crowd, where the crowd forms a scene. In the darkness of the movie theatre, cinema confers a secure duration and a protected stability to that spell that Flaubert had already recognized, in an era in which the spectator was nevertheless exposed to dangers:

> The drums sounded the attack. Shrill cries were heard, and shouts of triumph. The crowd surged backwards and forwards. Frederic, caught between two dense masses, did not budge; in any case, he was fascinated and enjoying himself tremendously. The wounded falling to the ground, and the dead lying stretched out, did not look as if they were really wounded or dead. He felt as if he were watching a play.[159]

In the rapid alternation of shots and lighting, as well as in the movements of the camera, cinema simply isolates this state of dangerous suspension, distributing ranks of dreamy Frederics across movie theatres; while

---

159 Gustave Flaubert, *Sentimental Education* (Robert Baldick and Geoffrey Wall trans) (London: Penguin, 2004), p. 311.

in every image it projects the living and fluctuating appearance of the crowd, it produces the real and inert, terrified or delighted crowd of spectators. It is no cabbalistic play with dates to say that cinema was born with the death of [Jean-Martin] Charcot; abandoned by its severe master, Grand Hypnotism could truly be reinvented in the Lumière brothers' workshop. The first to sense this was a philosopher: already in 1889, the classical arts appeared to Bergson as subtle hypnotic processes. Cinema's 'qualitative progress' was a powerful and irresistible common feeling; the seventh art was the art of suggestion as such. As Luis Buñuel remarked: 'Just watch people leaving a movie theatre; they're usually silent, their heads droop, they have that absentminded look on their faces'; when the melancholy multitude melts into the city, 'cinematographic hypnosis' acts on the spectator as 'a kind of fascination. Sometimes, watching a movie is a bit like being raped.'[160]

The conquest of the waking state, that is to say, the acquisition of class consciousness, the transformation of crowd into class, will thus consist of the opposite gesture, of a peculiar displacement, an 'entry' that simultaneously abolishes the point of view's exteriority and spectacular appearance.

Is this line of flight possible? Can we begin to trace it? From Frederic's standpoint alone, no, we cannot. To imagine a line, at least one other point is necessary.

**33.** Shy. He is different from them, aloof one might say. He says (as Kafka did to Brod): '[A] mob of friends [*Freundliche Masse*] is useful only in revolutions, when all

---

160 Luis Buñuel, *My Last Breath* (Abigail Israel trans.) (London: Fontana, 1985), p. 69.

act together and simply; but if what you have is only a small uprising by flickering light at a table, such friends will spoil it.'[161]

As Tarde wrote, with them he cannot feel at ease; he cannot 'adopt [the] manners and fashions [of that milieu], to speak its dialect, to copy its gestures'. In particular, he would never be able 'to abandon [himself] so completely that all consciousness of this self-abandonment is lost'.[162] More than a product of anxiety or disquiet, what makes him not very sociable, his shyness, is a small stubborn wakefulness. In which slumber would he not lose himself?

Tarde added that the crowd is an elementary form of identification, an inferior social fact. Society instead is a diffuse and continuous imitation. There are guiding ideas and brilliant supra-social individuals, standing out from the rest and attracting like magnetic poles while eliciting currents of imitation. So, there are always new adaptations. There is a vital and constant flow of adaptations to guiding ideas, which always generate new and inventive imitations. For Tarde, to invent is to adapt; to follow a current within the big magnetic field until it crosses another, and to resolve the contrast between them in the simplest (i.e. the more easily imitable) way, thus giving rise to a new pole towards which new currents can be rerouted. 'The social like the hypnotic state is only a form of dream, a dream of command and a dream of action. Both the somnambulist and the social man are possessed by the illusion that their ideas, all of which

161 Franz Kafka, 'Letter to Max Brod' (1904) in *Letters to Friends, Family, and Editors* (Richard and Clara Winston trans) (New York: Schocken, 1977), p. 13.

162 Gabriel Tarde, *The Laws of Imitation* (Elsie Clews Parsons trans.) (New York: Henry Holt, 1903), p. 86.

have been suggested to them, are spontaneous.'[163] The social is the unlimited sleep of inventive imitations.

The crowd, which follows anyone and does not invent anything, would thus be a sclerosis of this movement. But let's return to Taine's story: 'ten thousand, twenty thousand brigands had arrived . . . '. This first rumour engenders the crowd but it soon reveals itself as false. Then a second rumour begins to circulate: '[T]he danger . . . is coming from somewhere else.'[164] This is already an idea about the crowd. For the multitude coming back into its villages after the false alarm is a disappointed and, as it were, blocked mob, a *foule en impasse* bereft of any outlet; a barely acknowledged evidence (there are no brigands in sight) hindered its dissolution. The second rumour, which oversteps any certainty and resists all denials, is, at one and the same time, an imitation of the first rumour, an adaptation and an invention. Of what? Of unlimited danger. It could be noted that it is only thanks to this idea that the French peasants of 1789 really did return to their villages, that is, to society. In other words, this idea turns the crowd into a short-lived stage of society; thanks to it, unlimited society reabsorbs the crowd into itself; and the true alarmist voice, namely, the (not simply false but wholly invisible, always imminent and truly invented) danger unlimitedly regenerates society starting from the crowd. To quote Tarde again: 'It is for this reason, perhaps, that so-called savages, people who strongly rebel against assimilation and who are really unsociable, remain timid during their whole life. They are but partially subject to somnambulism.'[165]

---

163 Ibid., p. 77.

164 Tarde, 'Conviction and the Crowd', p. 236.

165 Tarde, *The Laws of Imitation*, p. 86 (translation modified).

34. Shyness is on the hither side of imitation. The genius is supra-social and attracts new flows of imitation. Solidarity wakes one up from the spell of prestige.

The inventive singularity of the *meneur* remained so essential to Tarde's model that a hypothetical society of geniuses—opposed to the crowd of the *menés* and deprived of any inventive capacity—was for him also marked by the threatening and corrosive shadow of anarchy, understood as the infinite proliferation of poles and consequent impossibility of any magnetic attraction, the definitive paralysis or absolute evil of socialization.

The anarchic component instead marks out the revolutionary class, which sees supra-social talent as the familiar product of the apparatuses of knowledge. Following a particular kind of inversion, in that class the leader does not emerge to then act as a pole of attraction. As Benjamin teaches us, his action instead consists in allowing himself to be immediately reabsorbed, forestalling any possible magnetism. One can think here of a type of genius that is never solitary as a new form of attention or a different way of perceiving, of the felicitous discovery of the unprecedented trait in each and every gesture qua invention. To be one of the hundred thousand: for in them nothing stops being singular; because there is no act that cannot be the inimitable act of solidarity, loosening and dissolving social ties within us.

Then, 'when all act together and simply', there appears the essence of revolutions and of every true revolt, indestructible even in its failure, both scattered and saved by memory. As Juan Goytisolo writes in *Para vivir aquí* [To Live Here]:

> For about six days there had not been a moment of rest. The city's rhythm of life had been suddenly altered and on the faces of the men and women walking along the pavements one could

read a firm sign of decision, of hope. A tacit solidarity united us all. We discovered we were not alone, and after twenty years of shame, that discovery stunned us. Our gazes crossed, and they were gazes of complicity. The most insignificant of life's gestures, like the very fact of walking, took on an unusual and almost miraculous character. People were tracing their everyday circuits silently, and this silence . . . [166]

was not menacing.

**35.** Marx's dialectic, as Fallot especially underscored, is a dialectic 'of the limit and unlimited, *ápeiron péiras*: the idea of the limit is as important for it as it was for the most advanced ancient materialism, that of Epicurus'.[167]

In *Marx et le machinisme* [Marx and Machinism], Fallot returns to the letter of *Capital*: 'Having reached a certain point in the development of production, the increase in the duration of the working-day, the principal means to obtain surplus value at the dawn of capitalism, in Marx's words "finds its limit".'[168] Capital will therefore aim at increasing the intensity of work. But not even this can grow infinitely; even the living labour-power of the worker possesses its objective limit. Thus 'for absolute surplus-value, the problem is the limit of the working-day; for relative surplus-value, it is the limit of necessary labour-time'.[169] The solution will be *productivity*, namely

166 Juan Goytisolo, *Para vivir aquí* (Cincinnati: AIMS International Books, 1977; original publication: Buenos Aires: Sur, 1960), p. 101.

167 Jean Fallot, *Marx et le machinisme* (Paris: Éditions Cujas, 1966), p. 178.

168 Ibid.

169 Ibid.

science as intellectual power of production; when duration and intensity reach their limits, science steps into
the unlimited. What is unlimited is thus the domination
of surplus-value, that is, of productivity and machines.

The basic technique of work shifts already contained
a hint of this. However, by welding one shift to the other
into one working day, it aimed at obliterating the limit
of duration, only to come up against the problem of
intensity. Now, fundamental to the concept of productivity is that it does not eliminate but, rather, includes (as
necessary rest or turn-taking) everything that formerly
lay beyond a limit. This is the 'intellectual power of production', where *power* [*potenza*] means the intellectual
capacity to absorb the limits of duration and intensity
into production itself; and where *intellectual* means that
there is no magic here, simply the new power [*forza*] of
machines. But prior to and facing the latter, there is a
power that does not let itself be frightened—even though
'Promethean shame', the shame in the face of technical
instruments studied by Günther Anders is no fantasy;[170]
it too would be nothing but the product of the selfsame
intellectual power, or better of the material-intellectual
domination of capital and surplus-value (structure, its
super-structural expressions, and the reflections of the
latter on the former). About 'Promethean shame', we can
also say with Marx: 'It does not come from the machines
themselves, but from their capitalist use!' Not that a good
use of the same products is possible; rather, precisely
because at the beginning there is *that* use and *those* products are the products and means of that use, the use cannot but be shameful.

---

170 Günther Anders, *Die Antiquiertheit des Menschen. I: Über die
Seele im Zeitalter der zweiten industriellen Revolution* (Munich: Beck,
1956).

This science of production is therefore an unlimited power in the precise sense suggested by Milner: the function of productivity in effect includes every instant among its possible variants, and there exists nothing (whether in terms of duration or intensity) or nobody ('reserve *army*' means reserve without limits where everyone is everyone else's reserve) which is exempt from its incessant production of meaning. It is here, on the plane of productivity, that Marx's affirmation that 'there is no limit to the working-day' cannot be denied—it defines exactly the function of productivity as a social function.

The Marxist function qua dialectical function will instead be to attain the antinomy *ápeiron péiras* knowing that only the unlimited limits the unlimited. The formula remains 'There is no instant of work that cannot be saved.' What does this mean? These are strange savings indeed. The word itself is shot through with irony. But is it just a word? More than the word is the principle, as real as it is ironic, of unlimited limitation. It's not a matter of duration or intensity here either. No doubt, even Lafargue had to admit a minimum amount of daily work. No doubt, in laying claim to *paresse*, laziness, he did not merely wish to restrict the working day to the bare minimum but to transform it into an activity entirely devoted to idleness, each of whose limited instant has idleness as its end. No doubt, *paresse* has dissolved the sad pair *travail-loisir*, work-leisure. And we should not forget another lesson of Milner's: the bourgeoisie in its current form, the waged bourgeoisie, is the class that converges around the *ideal*, namely, around that which 'obfuscates the difference in kind between rest, *loisir* and *otium*'.[171] There is nothing to object to when it comes to Lafargue's

---

171 Jean-Claude Milner, *Le Salaire de l'idéal. La théorie des classes et de la culture au XXᵉ siècle* (Paris: Éditions du Seuil, 1997), p. 54.

profound intelligence. If not, perhaps, exactly this: that between one idleness and another, there is always some work to be done, a work that is still 'the first means' and not 'the first need'; that there is indeed a remainder, that is to say, a division, a dichotomy or relation, but also an end as well as a pair of opposites—sadness and consolation, again in shifts.

The only answer to 'there is no limit to the working-day' will thus be 'there is not a single instant that cannot not be limited'. Unlimited limitation: this dialectical rather than ironic formula expresses the Marxist idea of the limit. And the idea of the limit, as Fallot suggests, is as important for Marxism as it had been for the materialism of Epicurus.

**36.** It is necessary thus to reconstruct the chain linking dialectic, solidarity, limit and Epicureanism. Following in Fallot's steps we need to recover the pleasure in solidarity, the hedonism of struggle.

In a by-no-means-eccentric passage from his *Pensée de l'Égypte antique* [The Thinking of Ancient Egypt], Fallot writes: 'Solidarity as a mass relationship is the outcome of a long path that allows the human being no longer to be fully incorporated into the organization of the economy.'[172]

Years earlier, Fallot concluded *Il piacere e la morte nella filosofia di Epicuro* [Pleasure and Death in the Philosophy of Epicurus] with a chapter on the 'reduction of desire', and in particular with some words on the Marxist modality of this reduction, which,

---

172 Jean Fallot, *La Pensée de l'Égypte antique* (Paris: Publisud, 1992), p. 121.

thanks to the union of theory and praxis, consists in gradually replacing our personal desires (for distinction, pre-eminence, possession, enjoyment) with a feeling for the needs of the masses. To fuse with the masses, to merge into the body of the masses—how many times have we heard these expressions? Objectively, they have a precise political meaning, for it is the masses who make history; but they also have a subjective, moral meaning—namely, that of reducing our personal and insignificant desires, dissolving them into the immense sea of the needs of the exploited and enslaved'.[173]

Fallot's *La Science de lutte de classe* [The Science of Class Struggle] contains a brief paragraph on 'ancient and modern hedonism and the needs of the masses'. Ancient materialism, which aimed at the satisfaction of natural and necessary needs, here becomes historical, and the very notion of nature is unthinkable when severed from that of social relations of production. The principles of Epicurean hedonism can thus be reached 'on the basis of other premises which endow them with a revolutionary meaning'—the satisfaction 'of everyone's natural needs, first and foremost of the producers: proletarian hedonism'.[174]

Earlier still, however, *Lutte de classe et morale marxiste* [Class Struggle and Marxist Morality], posed another

---

173 Jean Fallot, *Il piacere e la morte nella filosofia di Epicuro* (Sebastiano Timpanaro introd., Anna Marietti Solmi trans.) (Turin: Einaudi, 1977), p.112. This is the expanded, Italian version of Fallot's *Le Plaisir et la mort dans la philosophie d'Epicure* (Paris: Juillard, 1951).

174 Jean Fallot, *La Science de lutte de classe* (1973, unpublished manuscript); Italian translation: *Scienza della lotta di classe* (Ivano Spano ed.) (Verona: Bertani, 1974), p. 85.

problem: just like communism invents different relations of production from those based on property, so it is
necessary to affirm another morality that would take the
place of the morality founded on interest. In this sense,
the existence of solidarity needs to coincide with 'the very
existence of the proletariat whose exploitation is made
possible only by the demoralization, weariness and internal rivalry of its members, who individually strive to
bourgeois status, economically to desert (this is the term
repeatedly used by the young Marx) their own class (in
relation to wealth), politically to abandon the class struggle, morally to withdraw their solidarity'.[175] So it is not
just a matter of a subjective moral sense that accompa-
nies the concrete political one; but of revolution itself
as morality, against the morality of the bourgeois and
the immorality of the deserter. Is this a kind of moral
teaching then? In 1972, *Lutte de classe* was translated into
Italian. Fallot had added a preface which doubled as a
firm self-criticism:

> The 'mass' remains anonymous, undifferenti-
> ated [ . . . ]. A mass-Marxist would never have
> written a 'Marxist morality'; he would never
> have even contemplated it. To be able to think a
> Marxist morality (not to possess or follow it), it
> is necessary to think about oneself, to extrapo-
> late oneself as individual. [ . . . ] Mine was the
> error of an aesthete.[176]

No morality here and no teacher, if 'aestheticism'
means desertion, 'desertion' a desire to emerge from
anonymity, and 'anonymity' pleasure.

---

175 Antoine Brognard (Jean Fallot), *Lutte de classe et morale marxiste*
(Aubenas: Lienhart et Cie, 1968), p. 231.

176 Jean Fallot, *Lotta di classe e morale marxista* (Fabio Arcangeli
trans.) (Verona: Bertani, 1972), p. 15.

37. The history of biopower teaches us that the security paradigm which underlies contemporary *dispositifs* of control acts by projecting a variegated spectrum of fears; to govern means to manage desires while eliciting anxieties, thus to separate from our lives the phantasmagoria of a desirable or (it amounts to the same) redoubtable existence. In this way, 'every security is conquered from a prior insecurity and generates a new one'.[177] The formula defines a field of tension, the space of an uninterrupted battle. Fears and aspirations face off along the lines of social antagonisms. The latter are so many broad or narrowed bands, edges or compact zones, threadlike axes of symmetry between hopes and anxieties, unstable by-products of accumulated pressures. Instability, which nourishes every good government, is thus the matrix of the entire social space—the crowd is its purest manifestation. Pasquale Rossi had glimpsed this after a fashion when, in his *Sociologia e psicologia collettiva* [Collective Sociology and Psychology] (1904),[178] he had attributed a primary role and a synthetic character to crowd psychology among the other social sciences, and when before that (in *L'animo della folla* [The Soul of the Crowd], 1898) he represented society as a qualitatively homogenous continuum and its different formations as 'the rings of a chain, the first of which is the crowd while the last is the state'.[179] The so-called 'unstable aggregate' is in fact

177 Helmut Plessner, *Macht und menschliche Natur. Ein Versuch zur Anthropologie des geschichtlichen Weltansicht* (1931) in *Gesammelte Schriften*, V (Günter Dux, Odo Marquard, Elisabeth Ströker et al. eds) (Frankfurt: Suhrkamp, 2003), p. 198.

178 Pasquale Rossi, *Sociologia e psicologia collettiva* (Cosenza: Riccio, 1904).

179 Pasquale Rossi, *L'animo della folla* (Roma: Colombo, 1898), p. 102.

nothing other than an aggregation of instability itself—
whence its primacy.

Rereading Fallot today means learning how to
counter this suffocating perspective with a different strategy, the one announced in Athens by 'the philosopher
who was perhaps the most daring of all because he was
the most lucid'.[180] What is desire in the Epicurean vision?
And how does it arise? Desire is the absence of pleasure,
emerging where the immediacy of sensation and enjoyment is broken, giving rise to an unhappy and unquen-
chable thirst, to the fear of missed fulfilment or to
passions that are ultimately sedentary desires, desires
that 'have put on some pounds'.[181] It is thus necessary—
this is the first hedonistic principle—to rebel against all
separations, to recover pleasure in the wait for pleasure
itself, as well as in the satisfaction of every natural need.
For the basis of life itself is pure pleasure, the silence of
every desire and of every anxiety or passion. It is a question of cultivating a morality of enjoyment against a morbid Christian morality focused on the sufferings that
follow upon pleasure; it is a matter of attaining *ataraxia*
not by renouncing but by overcoming lust, of keeping the
stimulus within its limit in order for pleasure not to be
diminished, of slowing down pleasure in order to give
oneself over to it in a way the lustful could never do. For
the Epicurean, reaching the limit of pleasure means
freeing oneself from anxiety and illusions, becoming
wise and becoming philosophers. This entails possessing
a new idea of time, to cease confusing external time—
which is the relation between the movement of bodies—
with the time that is within us (the movement of our
sensations); it means knowing that no time survives our

---

180 Fallot, *Il piacere e la morte nella filosofia di Epicuro*, pp. 94–5.
181 Ibid., p. 20.

passing, only the relation of bodies and stars. If duration is not the purpose of life, one cannot be afraid of losing it. No duration, no anxiety. As Fallot wrote in the first version of *Le Plaisir et la mort dans la philosophie d'Épicure* (1951): 'Epicurus freed life from fate in order to unite it with pleasure. Death is no longer the final blow of a fate that does not exist.'[182] Where does this liberation manifest itself? In friendship, from which pleasure is inextricable because friendship 'is not external to our needs'.[183] Though one should not desire security, it may nevertheless be found in friendship, which is not reducible to utility. As Epicurus says: 'We do not so much need the help of our friends as the confidence of their help in need'.[184]

Now, for Fallot, the contemporary significance of Epicurean friendship and liberation is to be found in revolutionary solidarity. How are we to limit desire and to recover pure pleasure or life itself as pleasure in the midst of biopolitical domination in which every life instead becomes desirable? When the pressure of antagonisms empowers and nourishes desires, only an entirely contrary dynamic could attain their limit, and touch upon pleasure as such. It is precisely in solidarity, then, that the ancient materialist conception of nature, of natural life as pleasure, acquires a historical character. If the Epicurean hedonist knew that 'pleasure is not the end of desire but the effect of need when the latter is satisfied', the Marxist hedonist knows that to desire is to dread an unsatisfied need and that the very social *dispositif* that guarantees life and makes it desirable will never be able to give up on the more or less brutal

182 Fallot, *Le plaisir et la mort dans la philosophie d'Epicure*, p. 79.
183 Ibid., p. 64; *Il piacere e la morte nella filosofia di Epicuro*, p. 39.
184 Cited in ibid.

negation of needs. Seventeenth-century theorists had already affirmed that this negation is at the basis of every political economy. Pietro Verri, to mention just one, recognized in pain 'the prime mover' of the machinery of government. He therefore defined pleasure negatively, as the *'rapid cessation of pain'*.[185] It is with such conceptions that the hedonistic view of pleasure must be contrasted. It knows that where political economy dominates, there cannot be anything natural but only the mythologeme 'nature', nothing 'vital' but only the mythologeme 'life'. Therefore, to abolish any and all safety thresholds means recognizing that I will never stop desiring and fearing as long as my life will itself appear desirable; it thus means dialectically discovering the limit of my desire in the fulfilment of a need that will no longer be mine. Pleasure will only be a brief and appealing interval; there will be hope, dread, antagonism and myth until the satisfaction of a need is denied. For the same reason, however, there is no desire that cannot be limited, no fear that cannot be snuffed out in the unlimited sea of the needs of the subjugated and exploited. So, no altruism, just hedonism. No moralism but only the anonymity of pleasure.

To recap: where antagonism binds needs to desires, pleasure can be achieved only in loosening, action steeped in solidarity can only be hedonistic. Where every desire is the expression of the unlimited economy of insecurities, and every need impinges on other needs like a more anxious desire, hedonistic limitation can only take place amid the unlimited mass of needs; hedonism

185 Pietro Verri, *Sull'indole del piacere e del dolore* (1773) in *Edizione nazionale delle opere di Pietro Verri, III, 1: Discorsi e altri scritti degli anni Settanta* (Giorgio Panizza with Silvia Contarini, Gianni Francioni and Sara Rosini eds) (Rome: Edizioni di Storia e Letteratura, 2004).

and solidarity coincide in the loosening of the mass. Finally, if the unstable and compressed crowd is the matrix of the state, the revolutionary class as its internal loosening is the prelude of the 'without classes'—this is the expression of an absolute pleasure that is truly free of anxieties, the anarchic formula of social ataraxia.

**38.** What does Marx's worker do when he faces the capitalist? How does he clash with him? Just how can he make his own voice heard, transforming an issue that would otherwise be insignificant for capital into a true class confrontation? What is the first thing he affirms? Marx explains both the what and the how. Class struggle is also a question of form. The motto of the bourgeois humanist reads: 'Man, never say "I"!' The worker instead speaks in the first person singular. '*I want to be the one who administers my only property*, my labour-power, as a reasonable and parsimonious bursar, and I want to abstain from any mad profligacy.' We have seen how this idea of saving is profoundly ironic. Every reasonable economist, as Marx explains in the *Grundrisse*, always advises workers to save: '[T]he demand [is] that they should always hold to a minimum of life's pleasures and make crises easier to bear for capitalists etc. Maintain themselves as pure labouring machines and as far as possible pay their own wear and tear.'[186] Besides, it is obvious that if they were to follow that advice *as a rule*, really limiting consumption to a minimum, workers would only harm themselves: 'If he adopted wealth as his purpose, instead of making his purpose use value, [the worker] would then, therefore, not only come to no riches, but would moreover lose use value in the bargain.'[187]

---

186 Marx, *Grundrisse*, p. 286.
187 Ibid.

Now, class struggle must be rethought starting from this firm and sarcastic refusal of every 'savings' and every 'wealth'. This refusal is also a speaking in the first person and as such simultaneously expresses the *unconditional refusal of all mediations*. Wealth and mediation effectively form an inseparable dyad:

> It is important to note that wealth as such, i.e. bourgeois wealth, is always expressed to the highest power as exchange value, where it is posited as *mediator*, as the mediation of the extremes of exchange value and use value them-selves. This intermediary situation [*Mitte*] always appears as the *economic* relation in its complete-ness, because it comprises the opposed poles, and ultimately appears as a one-sidedly higher power *vis-à-vis* the extremes themselves.[188]

Thus, with one of his most powerful raids into the heart of the Hegelian system, Marx wrests 'wealth' from that development which through the very experience of the deepest alienation and sundering was meant to lead the Self back into itself. Here there is no 'noble con-sciousness' that recognizes in wealth the alienation of its 'Self as such', that glimpses 'its Self in the power of an estranged will'. It is instead mediation itself—the ecstasy of capital—that isolates and makes a spectacle of itself: '[T]he movement, or the relation, which *originally* appears as mediatory between the extremes necessarily develops dialectically to where it appears as mediation with itself, as the subject [*Subjekt*] for whom the extremes are merely its moments, whose autonomous presupposition it sus-pends in order to posit itself, through their suspension, as that which alone is autonomous.'[189] In a very telling

188 Ibid., p. 331.
189 Ibid., p. 332.

manner, at this point Marx draws the religious sphere closer to the more strictly economic one: Christ, the mediator between God and man, becomes more important than God, the saints more important than Christ and the priests more important than the saints; the same happens in the economy, for example, in commerce, where the wholesaler takes on the role of the dominant middle term. The 'extreme' figure of mediation is here the financier who places himself between the state and bourgeois society at its highest level of development.

This discovery of the autonomy of the intermediary moment in the materialist dialectic is tantamount in Marx to the replacement of the traditional formula 'capital-interest' with the critical one: 'capital-profit'. '*Wealth as such*' reveals itself as a higher form of mediation which, evermore distant from production, 'everywhere posits the lower form as labour, as mere source of surplus value'. The magical expression 'capital-interest' with its 'occult faculty to make a value differ from itself' concealed mediation; the formula 'capital-profit' destroys the magic of wealth.

The modalities of this illusion are nevertheless diverse. Many are the possible illusionists, as are their sometimes rather dark charms:

> Strangers were taken in front of the meanest possible, begrimed, yellowy, flat brick wall, with two rows of unadorned window-holes one above the other, and were exhorted with bated breath to behold and admire the simplicity of the headquarters of the great financial force of the day. The word THRIFT perched right up on the roof in giant gilt letters, and two enormous shield-like brass-plates curved round the corners on each side of the doorway were the only shining

spots in de Barral's business outfit. Nobody
knew what operations were carried on inside
except this—that if you walked in and tendered
your money over the counter it would be calmly
taken from you by somebody who would give
you a printed receipt.[190]

All the stolid, ruinous, final nullity of any dominant
middle or intermediary term is condensed in the figure
of de Barral from Joseph Conrad's 1913 novel *Chance*.
He 'was a mere sign, a portent. There was nothing in
him. Just about at that time the word Thrift became popular. You know the power of words.'[191] And ultimately,
through the not-exactly-vacant-but-swarming nullity of
the financier, through the sad numberless throng of the
defrauded, we can still glimpse labour.

In it is indeed de Barral—ultimately nothing but a
symbol—who can also assume the role of mediator-trade
unionist, administering, in more or less arcane negotia-
tions, savings that are insolvable by definition, namely,
the savings of one who is always, in Marx's formulation,
a 'virtual pauper'.[192] De Barral gladly takes leave from the
abodes of production but he does not remain hidden. Nor
can he be seen at what might be called true strikes,
choosing instead to take part only in inane triumphant
rallies: 'We have won the same salary as before, while
increasing our working hours!'—and the familiar, old
crowd of Melville's *Rich Man's Crumbs* (1854) applauds.

Instead, Marx's worker speaks in the first person,
for him or herself, unmoved by any interest in charity or

---

190 Joseph Conrad, *Chance: A Tale in Two Parts* (London: Methuen,
1914), pp. 71–2.

191 Ibid., p. 66.

192 Marx, *Grundrisse*, p. 604.

welfare, nor expecting it, refusing this 'thrift' and asking: 'You preach abstinence to me?' The question is addressed to the capitalist in the same way that it would be to any mediator, priest or watchman. It is precisely when they say 'I' that workers are in solidarity, removed from the dialectic of capital, already a class.

**39.** With the same gesture with which he framed the problem of the working day, Marx pushed the concept of population back into the foreground of bourgeoisie society. The polemic against Malthus, an author whom he openly despised, had a definite instrumental function, namely, to reprise the old theory of populations precisely where it is articulated from 'the brutal viewpoint of capital',[193] in order to free it from mythical presuppositions and ahistorical constants; to free the concept of *surplus population* from any sense that it is a 'homogenous fact';[194] and thus, to return to the concept of population so as to show that surplus populations are now produced in bourgeois society in a way 'which occurs in no earlier period of human history',[195] that is, in a way which is in keeping with 'the great historic quality of capital' that is 'the creation of surplus labour'.[196] The enigma of the self-production of a surplus population out of the existing population is in fact solved in the same way as the enigma of the self-valorization of capital—through capital's power of disposing of a determined quantity of unpaid labour, that is, of surplus labour.

193 Ibid., p. 605.

194 Ibid. (translation modified—the Nicolaus translation has '*of the same kind* in all the different historical phases of economic development').

195 Marx, *Capital, Volume 1*, p. 785.

196 Marx, *Grundrisse*, p. 325.

Marx explains that to surplus labour there corresponds a surplus population. The latter is a necessary
product of capitalist accumulation but is simultaneously
one of its preconditions; it is thus both a product and a
necessary condition for the development of the productive force of labour *within the limits of capitalist production*.
A sudden expansion (or contraction) of the scale of production, the vicissitudes of the industrial cycle, the power
and elasticity of machines, the increase of exchange
transactions and the progress of science all require the
greatest and most immediate availability of labour-power:
'In all such cases, there must be the possibility of suddenly throwing great masses of men into the decisive
areas without doing any damage to the scale of production in other spheres. The surplus population supplies
these masses.'[197] It is not necessary to insist on the contemporary resonance of these words. Population-space,
the political dominion of capital, always implies an
excess. Paris will always be insecure—overpopulation is
its product and precondition.

**40.** Eighteenth-century authors used to divide the notion
of population into just and true or false and apparent.
Marx shows that this division corresponds to the split of
the working-day into necessary and surplus labour. We
know that when the portion of surplus labour reaches its
maximum limit of duration, it, so to speak, turns back
and expands, limiting the time of necessary labour. This
is what relative surplus-value is, the increase of surplus
labour as the decrease of necessary labour; in other
words, as Marx explains, the continuous production of
a *superfluous labour-power*. In the *Grundrisse*, the law of

197 Marx, *Capital, Volume 1*, p. 785.

surplus population within the unlimited dominion of capital is set out as follows:

> Since the necessary development of the productive forces as posited by capital consists in increasing the relation of surplus labour to necessary labour, or in decreasing the portion of necessary labour required for a given amount of surplus labour, then [ . . . ] part of these labour capacities must become superfluous, since a portion of them suffices to perform the quantity of surplus labour for which the whole amount was required previously. [ . . . ] The decrease of relatively necessary labour appears as increase of the relatively superfluous labouring capacities—i.e. as the positing of surplus population.[198]

Now, introducing the concept of surplus value, Marx writes:

> Surplus value in general is value in excess of the equivalent. The equivalent, by definition, is only the identity of value with itself. [ . . . I]f the worker needs only half a working day in order to live a whole day, then, in order to keep alive as a worker, he needs to work only half a day. The second half of the labour day is forced labour; surplus-labour. What appears as surplus value on capital's side appears identically on the worker's side as surplus labour in excess of his requirements as worker, hence in excess of his immediate requirements for preserving his vitality [*Lebendigkeit*].[199]

---

198 Marx, *Grundrisse*, p. 609.

199 Ibid., p. 324 (translation modified).

When there is relative surplus value, when what is 'in excess' of need increases to the detriment of everything that is closely bound to need, it is a portion of *Lebendigkeit* that is worn away. In what sense? It is not a matter of the half day that could still be lived without working. That is already in the capitalist's hands, since absolute surplus value precedes its relative counterpart and the maximum limit of duration has already been reached. The portions of time that will be available now are not the same really free moments of that ideal 'before'; they are produced by relative surplus value itself. These portions are not liberated but rather they *occupy* a space, insisting on a certain temporality, superimposing themselves upon something else and limiting it in turn. Upon what? Once again, *Lebendigkeit*. Except that at the very moment when it is corroded and offended, this being alive ceases to belong to the singular individual. If what from the viewpoint of capital appears as surplus value is for the worker only surplus labour, then what from the viewpoint of capital is surplus population or industrial reserve army, is, from the viewpoint of the worker, class—as nothing but a product of surplus labour. Relative surplus labour and even more so *loisir* undermine the *Lebendigkeit* of others who belong to the class. In a less rudimentary definition, we can say that when there is relative surplus value this *Lebendigkeit* coincides with the exploited class as such. The living being of the worker becomes class.

41. In the dominion of capital, work produces poverty, along with a (surplus) population deprived of elementary necessities. This is why when the worker confronts the capitalist in the first person and pushes the struggle on the working day to the point of antinomy, he is already

in solidarity. When he instead remains on the hither side of the antinomy, he does not act in a revolutionary way, and there is no class. This second worker, who will obtain only poverty for himself and for others, belongs to the crowd. He does not really speak in the first person, acts under the influence of suggestion and is ruled by fear. But now even fear and suggestion disclose their mystery. And there is no Oedipus in sight. As the product of surplus value, surplus population itself produces that silent coalition about which Marx speaks in the first chapter of *Capital* on 'so-called primitive accumulation':

> The advance of capitalist production develops a working class which by education, tradition and habit looks upon the requirements of that mode of production as self-evident natural laws. The organization of the capitalist process of production, once it is fully developed, breaks down all resistance. The constant generation of a relative surplus population keeps the law of the supply and demand of labour, and therefore wages, within narrow limits which correspond to capital's valorization requirements. The silent compulsion of economic relations sets the seal on the domination of the capitalist over the worker.[200]

Contrary to what Emmanuel Levinas thought, if Marxism breaks the harmonious curve of this development, with all its dull fatalism, it is because it understands the situation in which man finds himself not as something that is 'added to him' but as 'the very foundation of his being'.[201] *Nothing is added to man from the*

---

200 Marx, *Capital, Volume 1*, p. 899.

201 Emmanuel Levinas, *Quelques réflexions sur la philosophie de l'hitlerisme* (1934) (Paris: Payot & Rivages, 1977); English translation:

*outside when his own being, his own* Lebendigkeit *is histor-ical.* Lebendigkeit is a pivotal word. Marx does not use *Leben*, which would already amount to a hypostasis, but, rather, a term near to *Lebhaftigkeit*, indicating the pure quality of the living being, namely, vivacity as the proper character and mode of being alive. That which 'is added' to man is precisely what appears as natural. Only fate is parasitic. But the secret of *Lebendigkeit*—its historical a priori—is deposited in and revealed by relations of production. In Marx, there is neither biologism nor hyposta-sis of life, not even in the guise of an original sharing, of being as being in common, of a sharing of life as such. Life as such is a myth, unlike solidarity. Once again, we can say that under conditions of capitalist exploitation, until there is relative surplus value, solidarity is class *Lebendigkeit.*

Surplus population, the industrial reserve army, thus presses on the crowd which is prey to the most danger-ous stupefaction. But—in the Marxist countermove—surplus population is nothing but class and silent compulsion can be answered and opposed by distention, by 'mute solidarity'.

'There must be something besides sacrifice.' To return to Epicurus and Fallot, the basis of life is pure pleasure, the silence of all desire, as well as of every anx-iety or passion. Estrangement, which leads the single individual to renunciation, transforms the individual into a class. Only in struggle is there no longer any surplus population. The offended and mutilated living being, *Lebendigkeit* as the basis or vitality of life, urges forward in solidarity to the 'without classes'.

'Reflections on the Philosophy of Hitlerism' (Seán Hand trans.), *Critical Inquiry* 17(1) (1990): 67.

**42.** 'Large-scale industry concentrates in one place [*endroit*] a crowd of people unknown to one another.' Here the word 'place' (*endroit*) does not just point to the familiar walls of the factory; instead, it gives a wholly new meaning to the words 'factory' and 'walls'. It affirms the principle whereby what is valid within the workshop is also valid within society (Marx's formula, we could hazard, finds in the concept of 'abstract diagram' its most rigorous interpretation).

We have already recalled Jesi's words about revolt and the city but not yet those of Max Horkheimer from the last days of the Weimar Republic:

> As long as someone stays at the center of society, i.e., as long as he occupies a respected position and does not come into conflict with society, he does not discover what it really is. [ . . . ] The way the police occasionally treat the workers during an uprising or beat the imprisoned unemployed with the butts of their rifles, the tone the factory porter uses with the man looking for work, the workhouse and the penitentiary, all these function as the limits that disclose the space in which we live.[202]

All these violences and voices animate the first volume of *Capital*, echoing, for instance, in the pages on the depreciation of labour-power through the replacement of 'mature labour-power by immature, male by female',[203] or in those dedicated to 'factory legislation', to the commissions of inquiry in which workers are called to testify before juries formed of their own bosses: 'The

202 Max Horkheimer, *Dawn and Decline: Notes, 1926–1931 and 1950–1969* (Michael Shaw trans.) (New York: The Seabury Press, 1978), p. 76.

203 Marx, *Capital, Volume 1*, p. 788.

mode of examining the witnesses reminds one of the cross-examination of witnesses in English courts of justice, where the advocate tries, by means of impudent, confusing and unexpected questions, to intimidate and confound the witness, and to give a forced meaning to the answers thus extorted.'[204]

Even in the traces left by these hesitant voices, the Marxist paradigm of the *endroit* continues to this day to reveal the limits of social space. Regulating, managing or administering migratory flows, tacitly approving, letting be, simply assisting or voting—all of these are more or less passive and respectable functions; and the conditions on the basis of which they can operate are the same that unleash the worst reaction and racist hatred. But non-contradictory democratic functions are increasingly revealed to have a clear affinity with the behaviour of a vindictive crowd. Or, rather, this same obvious fact now stands like an impenetrable curtain, a kind of defensive lining for those who tarry prudently in the very middle of society.

A classical model of social formations was valid once upon a time: when the first, relatively small and closed circle, alien and antagonistic to neighbouring circles becomes bigger, when, with the words of Simmel, 'the group grows [ . . . ] to the same degree the group's direct, inner unity loosens, and the rigidity of the original demarcations against others is softened through mutual relations and connections'.[205] Both the state and Christianity, corporations and political parties, can be understood as developing in accordance with this general

---

204 Marx, *Capital, Volume 1*, p. 626.

205 Georg Simmel, 'The Metropolis and Mental Life' (1903) in *Simmel on Culture: Selected Writings* (David Frisby and Mike Featherstone eds) (London: Sage, 1997), p. 180.

schema of cohesion and ever-wider proximities. But an overturning was foreseeable, for sudden contraction shares the same logic. So, spatial proximity, that physical nearness that from Tarde to Canetti has always been recognized as the crowd's necessary precondition, is once again reaffirmed in the rhetoric of soil as the perennial source of life, shared by the group—a domestic soil or *endroit sécuritaire* that can be either regional or national, Italian or European, that may take the form of a community, a large or small, besieged and well-guarded Carinthia. Here we find the compressed throng, ready to explode and dissolve, which must always 'fight for its life', 'constantly "against" others'. In the outlook belonging to the crowd, ever-larger foreign masses press incessantly at the gates. Everything is a play of density and the enemy will suddenly be the closest neighbour. But from a point of view which is not that of the crowd, one alien from mythologies of security, political space is instead revealed as a vast mottled surface: according to Dèznai's model, urbanization is complete, 'the fight for internal equilibrium and urban security' is at work everywhere and one can observe more or less intense patches, compressions, small embattled families raising barriers of every kind.[206]

To this day, in all its forms, the 'real civil war' cannot but be the dissolution of biopolitical borders themselves, a loosening of the interests on the basis of which even Deleuze and Guattari's slogan will allow itself to be overturned: *il y a toujours la carte variable de la classe sous la reproduction des masses*—beneath the reproduction of the masses there is always the variable map of class.[207]

206 Deznài, 'L'activité intellectuelle des villes', p. 526.

207 ['Beneath the self-reproduction of classes, there is always a variable map of masses' ('*Il y a toujours one carte variable des masses sous la reproduction des classes*'). Gilles Deleuze and Félix Guattari,

**43.** Every revolutionary gesture is for Benjamin 'a question of technique', understood as the capacity to dominate critical instants, moments of maximum danger: '[I]f the abolition of the bourgeoisie is not completed by an almost calculable point [ . . . ] all is lost. Before the spark reaches the dynamite, the lighted fuse must be cut.'[208]

It is a matter of acting before the crowd, with its reactive hate, can explode. This is the decisive instant, where new compressions can take the place of loosenings. We are dealing with mutable phenomena, phenomena in movement; and technique itself (Benjamin is also thinking of cinema) is a phenomenon in movement. There is, of course, no shortage of examples and we know that in extremely critical situations, even within the seemingly most compact mass something can happen— in one direction or another.

A first case is the one analysed by Bruno Bettelheim and concerns the concentration camp. The Nazis discover an escape attempt, so they gather the inmates in the open square and begin one of their interminable role calls. A blizzard is blowing and the prisoners have already worked outdoors for twelve hours, with almost no food.

> After more than twenty prisoners had died of exposure the discipline broke down. Open resistance was impossible. [ . . . ] Therefore, the individual as such had to disappear in the mass. Threats by the guards became ineffective [ . . . ]

*A Thousand Plateaus: Capitalism and Schizophrenia* (Brian Massumi trans.) (Minneapolis: University of Minnesota Press, 1987), p. 221.]

208 Walter Benjamin, 'One-Way Street' in *Selected Writings, Volume 1, 1913–1926* (Marcus Bullock and Michael W. Jennings eds) (Cambridge, MA: Harvard University Press, 1996), p. 470.

it was as if what happened did not "really" happen to oneself. There was psychologically, and in experience, a split between the figure to whom things happened and the prisoner himself who did not care and was just vaguely interested, a detached observer. Unfortunate as the situation was, the prisoners then felt free from fear as individuals and powerful as a mass because "not even the Gestapo can kill us all tonight". [ . . . ] The extremeness of the situation kept the individual from protecting himself and forced him into mass formation. [ . . . ] Before this change in attitude took place [ . . . ] they had been shocked and weakened by the inability to help dying comrades. Once they abandoned hope for their personal existence, it became easier for them to act heroically and help others. Another factor was that because they had become free of fear, the SS had actually lost its power.[209]

Once again, it is not a question of the 'reversal of the fear of being touched' but of something that exceeds even this phenomenon and the ensuing effect of relief that would be 'most striking where the density of the crowd is greatest'.[210] What is at stake here is a paradoxical transformation of the mass itself: an absence of fear reached at the moment of extreme danger, and in the most intense physical proximity, namely, the one imposed in the concentration camp, a sort of overcoming by excess of density itself. The mass, already formed and framed by fear, here becomes even more cohesive—so cohesive

209 Bruno Bettelheim, *The Informed Heart* (London: Penguin, 1991[1960]), pp. 137–8.
210 Canetti, *Crowds and Power*, p. 16.

that the individual, unable to put up any resistance, completely disappears into it. Now the mass' function is no longer the correlate of the function of the individual. The individual is no longer faced by the collective, because he is no longer an individual. Unlike the crowd brought together by panic, in which anxious loneliness finds its only comfort, this mass in solidarity is without fear because no one has anything to fear for himself any longer.

However, the simple temporary overturning of fear into its apparent opposite will always take place. For,

> the problem of fear is a difficult problem. The majority of people are afraid and consider only self-assured alarmists to be dangerous. [ . . . ] And as for those who are already half-aware, when they gather in the thousands, they forget that they have assembled in order to fear together, and to do something against those who have made them afraid. In fact, as soon as a hundred thousand come together, an enjoyable popular festival takes place. The sausages come out. [ . . . ] And then the guitars. And when these begin, so does collective stupidity.[211]

The reason why those people came together was the threat of total destruction. 'But when thousands of people get together, courage is automatically activated. In the melee where they wallow, they soon forget about Chernobyl.'[212] This not-very-admirable courage, of which [Günther] Anders speaks, is the panic in the face of the fear that is triggered in keeping with an entirely

211 Günther Anders, *Gewalt—ja oder nein. Eine notwendige Diskussion* (Munich: Knaur, 1987), p. 27.

212 Ibid.

predictable automatism. Its 'fuse' is still the fear of losing the world. But, for this mass, the loss of the world is *still only a fear* and thus, ultimately, a small individual fear. It is a petty fear, and petty is the ego that experiences it faced with the event that caused the fear in the first place. But the 'collective' courage into which it is converted is the most violent, because it prolongs and consolidates the threat; it dissimulates the threat and thus renders it all the more imminent. Before Hiroshima, before becoming the philosopher of the world without men, Anders was the philosopher of man without the world. Perhaps the production of a world without men can happen only as the work of men who have—or in any case, believe they have—a world and who are therefore afraid of losing it, while it can be fought only by 'men without a world'. Anders was a pupil of Heidegger and to a certain extent the theme of the loss of the world is of Heideggerian origin. Likewise, *Being and Time* orbits in its own way around that problem of estrangement which was 'in the air' (as Lukács later remarked) in the years of *History and Class Consciousness*. In a polemic with Heidegger, however, Anders had once written:

> *The expression 'man without world' defines a class condition.* The assertion—understood by Heidegger as [ . . . ] universally valid—according to which *Dasein* or being-there (as man's specific being) means *eo ipso* 'being-in-the-world', is to be referred exclusively to man as belonging to the dominant class. [ . . . ] Anyone who objects by saying that 'the world of poverty' is fundamentally a 'world' adopts a completely empty concept of world and does not deserve an explicit rebuttal, but merely that mockery which Marx reserved for Stirner, when he remarked that the latter would probably not have hesitated

to define the starving man as 'the owner of his
own hunger'.[213]


44. 'The propertied class and the class of the proletariat
present the same human self-estrangement. But the former class feels at ease and strengthened in this self-
estrangement [ . . . ]. The latter feels annihilated in
estrangement; it sees in it its own powerlessness.'[214]

Even the analysis of this second form of estrangement required the theoretical refinement of the *Pheno-
menology of Spirit*. As the young Lukács noticed, however,
grafting the Hegelian dialectic back onto Marx—and
turning Hegel into a revolutionary Marxist—produced
not a simple syncretism but a philosophical corpus that
attracts and unites in itself elements that are alien to one
another, and which becomes as brilliant as it is difficult
to master.

Starting from a Hegelian principle, therefore, something completely different is introduced: its figure is that
of the *leap*. The term is indeed still Hegelian: 'the *leap*
[ . . . ] this transition is *only thinking*' [*Der Sprung . . . dies
Übergehen ist nur Denken*],[215] but in Lukács it appears
completely transformed—it retains the not-so-implicit
mark of Kierkegaard and is also, above all, the Marxist,
revolutionary leap 'from the kingdom of necessity to the
kingdom of freedom'.

---

213 Günther Anders, *Mensch ohne Welt. Schriften zur Kunst und
Literatur* (Munich: Beck, 1984), p. *xiii*.

214 Marx and Engels, *The Holy Family*, p. 36.

215 G. W. F. Hegel, *The Encyclopaedia Logic: Part I of the Encyclopaedia of Philosophical Sciences, with the Zusätze* [1830] (T. F. Geraets,
W. A. Suchting and H. S. Harris trans) (Indianapolis, IN: Hackett,
1991), §50, p. 95.

If *History and Class Consciousness* really intended to 'restore the nature of Marx's theories by renovating and extending Hegel's dialectics and method',[216] this renovation and extension could only be reached once again through Marx: '[P]roletarian revolutions [ . . . ] criticise themselves constantly, interrupt themselves continually in their own course, come back to the apparently accomplished in order to begin it afresh, deride with unmerciful thoroughness the inadequacies, weaknesses and paltrinesses of their first attempts.'[217] This famous passage from the 'Eighteenth Brumaire' must be kept in mind in order to grasp Lukács' key definition (in which the Hegelian *Prozess* still echoes, albeit distortedly):

> [T]his leap does not consist of one unique act which without a transition brings about with lightning speed this, the greatest transformation in the history of mankind. [ . . . ] The leap is rather a lengthy, arduous process. Its essence is expressed in the fact that on every occasion it denotes *a turning in the direction of something qualitatively new.*[218]

The leap is a long process that in turn proceeds through leaps. One of these is the conflict over the working day: if a strike is truly such, it cannot in any way lead to a settlement, reproducing the capitalist relationship after some kind of adjustment. It cannot because if it is a real strike, it is, as a leap, always *turned towards something qualitatively new.* As Lukács recalled in

216 Lukács, *History and Class Consciousness*, p. *xxi*.

217 Karl Marx, 'The Eighteenth Brumaire of Louis Bonaparte' in Karl Marx and Friedrich Engels, *Collected Works, Volume 11* (London: Lawrence & Wishart, 1979), pp. 106–7.

218 Lukács, *History and Class Consciousness*, p. 250.

his 1967 preface to the republished *History and Class Consciousness*: 'My interest in Sorel was aroused by Ervin Szabó, the spiritual mentor of the Hungarian left-wing opposition in Social Democracy.'[219]

**45.** For Lukács, among the weapons of the proletariat, 'historical materialism is, of course, pre-eminent'.[220] For Benjamin, materialism is more precisely a technique requiring 'presence of mind'.[221]

First in Lukács and then in Benjamin, we find the same critique of bourgeois historicism and of its concept of atemporal historical truth.

Lukács explains how this conception is incapable of mastering process and must consequently suppress it, presenting historical data as eternal truths; alternatively, in keeping with a complementary strategy, 'everything meaningful or purposive [must be] banished from history'.[222] In this regard, Lukács quotes Leopold von Ranke's dictum according to which 'every age is "equally close to God"' [*Gott gleich nahe ist*]—here where every epoch has reached its own perfection, process is once again expunged.

Working on the theses of 'On the Concept of History', Benjamin also cites Ranke but in a way that marks his distance from *History and Class Consciousness*: 'If every epoch is immediately in relation to God (*jede Epoche ist unmittelbar zu Gott*), it is such only as the messianic time

219 Ibid., p. *x*.

220 Ibid., p. 223.

221 Benjamin, *The Arcades Project*, p. 476.

222 Lukács, *History and Class Consciousness*, p. 48.

of a preceding epoch'.[223] Like revolution for Marx, for Benjamin, too, history is a dialectical leap. But this leap is now so emancipated from process and from every tendency towards an end that even a dictum from Ranke is suited to it. Now the dialectical evolution towards self-consciousness is halted. For Benjamin, the existence of a classless society is not thinkable at the same time as the struggle for it. But just when every teleological relation is broken, every present—on the basis of the same idea of classless society—can become the time of a messianic judgement on a preceding epoch. And despite all attempts to expunge or conceal the theme of class struggle, Benjamin's stance remains clear: 'The subject of historical knowledge is the struggling, oppressed class itself' (Thesis XII); 'What characterizes revolutionary classes at their moment of action is the awareness that they are about to make the continuum of history explode' (Thesis XV).[224] This is the leap (*Sprung*) in the interpretation of Benjamin who transcribes the words of Marx and Engels against Bruno Bauer and the latter's idea of critical consciousness:

> The holy father of the church will be greatly surprised when judgment day overtakes him [ . . . ] a day when the reflection of burning cities in the sky will mark the dawn; when together with the 'celestial harmonies' the tunes of 'La Marseillaise' and 'Carmagnole' will echo in his ears accompanied the the requisite roar of cannon, with the guillotine beating time; when

223 Walter Benjamin, *Gesammelte Schriften I.1* (Rolf Tiedemann and Hermann Schweppenhäuser eds) (Frankfurt: Suhrkamp, 1991), p. 1174.

224 Benjamin, 'On the Concept of History', pp. 394–5.

the infamous 'masses' [*verruchte* '*Masse*'] will shout, 'Ça ira, ça ira!' and suspend [*aufhebt*] 'self-consciousness' by the lamppost.[225]

The class may seem like a crazed crowd, or it may appear dormant, incapable of gathering up its strength. Masses are, by definition unpredictable. Benjamin too had been a passionate reader of Sorel.

**46.** This was in fact the book's crude and intriguing prophecy: that henceforth popular myths, or better, myths trimmed for the masses, would be the vehicle of political action-fables, chimeras, phantasms that needed to have nothing whatever to do with truth, reason, or science in order to be productive nonetheless, to determine life and history [ ... ] the book [ ... ] dealt with violence as the triumphant counterpart of truth'.[226]

This is how Thomas Mann stigmatizes the *Reflections on Violence* in the thirty-fourth chapter of *Doctor Faustus*. It was from this passage that Karl Kerényi drew his celebrated distinction between 'genuine myth' and 'technicized myth'.

Literary fiction is the screen which, under the name of Serenus Zeitblom, counteracts direct trivialization and allows the aristocratic Mann to treat even crude prophesies with refined *sprezzatura*. His words on Sorel—which would be quite disputable in a targeted treatment—are

225 Marx and Engels, quoted in Benjamin, *The Arcades Project*, p. 652.

226 Thomas Mann, *Doctor Faustus: The Life of the German Composer Adrian Leverkühn as Told by a Friend* (John E. Woods trans.) (New York: Vintage, 1999), pp. 385–6.

true here precisely to the extent that they are generic and, while not addressing the letter of Sorel's doctrine, they treat the reality of his bad vulgarization with great exactitude.

Schmitt could not be as subtle. Having cited a speech by Mussolini ('our myth is the nation, the great nation'), in 'Die politische Theorie des Mythos' [Political Theory of Myth] (1923), he smugly observes: 'The fact that anarchist authors had discovered the irrationality of the mythic starting from their anti-authoritarian and anti-unitary hostility could not impede them from collaborating in the foundation of a new authority, of a new feeling for order, discipline and hierarchy.'[227]

We can also add Mircea Eliade's voice to the chorus:

> It was said [ . . . ] of the General Strike, that this was one of the rare myths created by the modern world. But this was a misunderstanding: it was supposed that an *idea*, accessible to a considerable number of individuals and therefore 'popular', could become a *myth* for the simple reason that its realization was projected into a more or less remote future. But that is not the way myths are 'created'. The general strike might be an instrument of political combat, but it has no mythical precedents, and that alone is enough to exclude it from mythical status.[228]

Mann and Kerényi agree with Schmitt about the possibility of a political use of irrational elements and

---

227 Carl Schmitt, 'Die politische Theorie des Mythus' (1923) in *Positionen und Begriffe im Kampf mit Weimar-Gempf-Versailles, 1923–1939* (Hamburg: Hanseatische Verlagsanstalt, 1940), p. 17.

228 Mircea Eliade, *Myths, Dreams, and Mysteries: The Encounter between Contemporary Faiths and Archaic Realities* (Philip Mairet trans.) (New York: Harper & Row, 1975), p. 25.

ultimately about bringing Sorel and Mussolini closer
together; but they do not agree with Schmitt regarding
the use of the terms 'myth' and 'mythic', which for them
are strictly inapplicable to Sorel. Mann and Kerényi agree
with Eliade on the exclusion of the general strike from
the sphere of myth but they could not agree with him
about the essence of the myth itself. By denying the singularity of the anarchist phenomenon (and, as Schmitt
does, assimilating it to fascism), denying the mythic quality of the strike (as does Eliade), or denying both (like
Mann and Kerényi), these three discordant voices converge on one point: they all tend to deny what for Sorel
remains essential, namely, the relationship of exclusive
co-implication between myth and the general strike.

47. And yet the advice 'not to hypostatise' myth as though
it were a concrete substance did come from Kerényi.
This correct advice must also be valid for reading the
*Reflections on Violence.*

What does 'myth' mean here? In the first place, not
utopia. For Sorel, utopia, as wielded by bourgeois trade-
unionism, is something akin to Kerényi's 'technicized
myth'. It is an artefact, a product of intellectual labour,
'the work of theorists who, after observing and discussing
the facts, seek to establish a model to which they can
compare existing societies'; utopia is both 'a combination
of imaginary institutions'[229] and a *description* of human
relations seen in their more desirable condition, but it is
useful to much less appealing political solutions.

Philosophy is the opposite of every 'intellectual
labour'. As Bergson said in *An Introduction to Metaphysics*:

229 Georges Sorel, *Reflections on Violence* (Jeremy Jennings ed.)
(Cambridge: Cambridge University Press, 2004[1908]), p. 27.

'To philosophize [ . . . ] is to invert the habitual direction of the work of thought'.[230] And myth can only be understood here in accordance with Bergson's philosophy which Sorel took quite literally. In myth, truly free action expresses itself. In a creative inversion of social time, it draws on and deploys itself as pure duration. As Bergson argued:

> Hence there are finally two different selves, one of which is, as it were, the external projection of the other, its spatial and, so to speak, social representation. [. . .] But the moments at which we thus grasp ourselves are rare, and that is just why we are rarely free. The greater part of the time we live outside ourselves [. . .] we speak rather than think; we 'are acted' rather than act ourselves. To act freely is to recover possession of oneself, and to get back into pure duration.[231]

Unlike utopia, in Sorel, myth cannot be manufactured for the masses because, being essentially new, it does not recognize any readymade collective just waiting to welcome it.

Kerényi based his life as a scholar on the distinction between myth and its fables, that is to say, mythologies— the only materials that can be historically appraised. With a similar gesture, Cesare Pavese warns us that 'you must be careful not to confuse myth with its past or present poetic versions; myth precedes the expression given to it, it is not that expression. With respect to myth, we are justified in speaking of a content distinct from the

---

230 Henri Bergson, An Introduction to Metaphysics (T. E. Hulme trans.) (New York and London: G.P. Putnam's Sons, 1912[1903]), pp. 69–70.

231 Henri Bergson, Time and Free Will: An Essay on the Immediate Data of Consciousness (F. L. Pogson trans.) (Mineola, NY: Dover, 2001[1889]), pp. 231–2.

form.'[232] But if Sorel does not mix up the two levels, it is because for him the distinction does not exist: myth does not precede the strike; it is the strike itself. Like one of those rare instants in which, according to Bergson, the free and conscious individual would grasp himself, in Sorel's *Reflections on Violence*, myth is the creative event in which the collective comes into contact with itself. If 'there are no two identical moments in the life of the same conscious being',[233] a moment that is both collective and truly new cannot arise in the external socialized environment where every being loses itself. On the contrary, it implies the destruction of existing society. Myth, which does not constitute a presupposition, has no precedents: far from being produced for the pre-compressed fascist mass, it is not resurrected as a 'technically fitted-out archaism'[234] but realizes itself only in loosening, as the unique appearance of the revolutionary class.

**48.** 'Not only is there no existent that can or must constitute a limit or an exception, but henceforth the society-function includes among its possible variables any existent whatsoever, human or nonhuman, animate or inanimate. There exists nothing and no one for whom the function ceases to produce meaning. There exists nothing and no one that can suspend society'.[235]

Obviously, the reactive crowd does not suspend society and neither do the dangerous criminalized individual

232 Cesare Pavese, 'Del mito, del simbolo e d'altro' (1943–44) in *Feria d'Agosto* (Turin: Einaudi, 2002[1946]), p. 150.

233 Bergson, *An Introduction to Metaphysics*, p. 12.

234 Guy Debord, *The Society of the Spectacle* (Donald Nicholson-Smith trans.) (New York: Zone Books, 1995), p. 77 (translation modified).

235 Milner, *Les Penchants criminels*, p. 23.

or the conformist bourgeois. But there exists the revolutionary class which destroys society. If the form of the latter extends into the form of money, and if the form of money and that of society communicate in the unlimited, then—as we saw with Marx—the revolutionary strike that suddenly surges up makes the very reasons of the commodity its own. It twists and turns them, revealing their antinomy, enlisting the magical and unlimited virtue of money into a totally new conflict where force faces force.

In this sense, according to its radical immanence in the commodity, the revolutionary class is not reducible to 'the concept of the political'; it does not experience the contrast with the alien nation or people; it does not affirm and maintain itself in a latent war against its enemy but exists only in the destruction of itself, as of all classes. It confronts the capitalist in the first person but with the irony of one who knows that his claims are so radical that it is no longer possible to envisage someone before whom they must be justified. If the class and its struggles demand a completely new temporal sequence, albeit one to which they cannot belong, the 'classless society' is no longer the 'organizing point for a political vision of the world'.[236] In this time, there is no longer a life that is to be integrated into a society without limits but, rather, an already unlimited and immediately social life, that is, a life that cannot in any way become *sociable*.[237]

In this time, space is also completely transformed. Paris is no longer Paris, nor Rome, nor Parma, while Parma is no longer Parma, nor Modena. Yes, the unlimited of society is a dream which, as Delfini has shown,

236 Ibid., p. 21.
237 [In French in the original.]

does not cease being inhabited by other and different dreams. But it is in the conflict over the working day that the unlimited ends; it is only in this conflict, a true civil war, that Paris really alters its visage: '[I]n the final analysis, only the revolution creates an open space for the city. [ . . . ] Revolution disenchants the city.'[238]

**49.** Benjamin's note on class, which isolates this messianic possibility from the mass itself, that is, from the compressed quintessence of society, retains even today all the force that Adorno recognized in it. In its original context, the essay on the reproducibility of art, it referred to the opportunities offered by cinematographic technique and to their counter-revolutionary transformation at the hands of capital. According to Benjamin, man's self-estrangement had reached a 'highly productive' stage in cinema. For a film actor, it becomes an essentially different phenomenon from the one produced on a theatre stage. This is because the image of the actor performing in front of the camera is by that very token exposed to the mass and transported before the mass 'who will control it'. But the latter is 'not visible, not present' yet—like in an upside-down Panopticon, where the hidden guards are a multitude and the prisoner stands alone in their presence—and this 'invisibility heightens the authority of their control'.[239]

As Benjamin goes on to say: 'It should not be forgotten, of course, that there can be no political advantage derived from this control until film has liberated itself from the fetters of capitalist exploitation.'[240] While this

238 Benjamin, *The Arcades Project*, p. 422.
239 Benjamin, 'The Work of Art', p. 113.
240 Ibid.

exploitation endures, instead, every possibility is systematically obstructed by a special bewitched curtain. The 'cult of the movie star' acts so as to 'preserve that magic of personality which has long been no more than the putrid magic of its own commodity character', while 'its counterpart, the cult of the audience, reinforces the corruption by which fascism is seeking to supplant the false consciousness of the masses.'[241]

In this 'corruption' we can glimpse the dangerous crowd, just as in the movie star's gaze there flickers the old 'charisma' of Tarde and Le Bon. But if fascism brings the critical and highly productive stage of estrangement back to the pair celebrity-mass, the prestigious leader-crowd, the answer to this danger is once again a technical question.

Béla Balázs drew attention to the capacity of cinema to develop

'typing' of class faces and facial expressions. Not stereotyped figures such as the 'over-refined degenerate aristocrat' contrasted with the 'coarse, powerful labourer'. We know that these were rough generalizations and the close-up tore off these primitive masks. Behind the external, conventional characteristics, the close-up revealed the hidden, impersonal class traits in individual faces.[242]

Balázs recalls the images from Dovzhenko's *Arsenal* (1929):

---

241 Ibid.

242 Béla Balász, *Theory of the Film (Character and Growth of a New Art)* (Edith Bone trans.) (London: Dennis Dobson, 1952[1949]), p. 82.

The scene shows the lull before the storm, the storm being the rising in Kiev. [ . . . ] Now in a series of brief scenes the film shows a cross-section of the social body of a whole city [ . . . ] unmistakably showing their class and showing it immanently in individual physiognomies; showing not man in his social class, but social class in men.[243]

Here a technical solution inaugurates a new phys-iognomic, finally untied from the subject and his psychology. By discovering class relations, that is, social relations, behind the aura of the movie star, it loosens the masses and blocks the constitution of the crowd. The public, the mass that gazes at this new experiment on the screen is as such a limit-phenomenon; it does not 'contemplate' but instead exercises its control over the social situation. It is 'loosened' in a very special way, and comes to know its distension only in struggle. What's more, even the image transported in front of a similar class is filmed by the machine and moves on the screen in conditions that are completely incomparable to the notion of a spectacle bestowed by capital. For, along with the cult of the movie star, the cult of the audience is also destroyed. In *this* kind of film, the relationship that links the star to the audience, and according to which he must adhere to the mass in order to lead it, is both exceeded and overcome.

When communist *artisans* [*Handwerke*] associate with one another, theory, propaganda, etc., is their first end. But at the same time, as a result of this association, they acquire a new need—the need for society—and what appears as a

---

243 Ibid., pp. 82–3.

means becomes an end. [ . . . ] Such things as smoking, drinking, eating, etc., are no longer means of contact or means that bring them together. Association, society and conversation, which again has association as its end, are enough for them; the brotherhood of man is no mere phrase with them, but a fact of life, and the nobility of man shines upon us from their work-hardened faces.[244]

This is not Balázs. It is Marx (from the *Manuscripts* of 1844). For in class solidarity, in which there can be no cult, in which the face of the proletarian leader is reabsorbed into the face of the class, those faces are both knowing and known, gazing out and gazed upon.

In 1915, Vachel Lindsay devoted some pages of his *The Art of the Moving Picture* to D. W. Griffith's *The Birth of a Nation*. Lindsay coined the term 'Crowd Picture' for this hateful masterpiece, a Ku Klux Klan apologia that on 'the films, as in the audience [ . . . ] turns the crowd into a mob'.[245] In particular, in the scene that reconstructs Abraham Lincoln's assassination, the fake audience in the fake Ford's Theatre rises up as though seized by panic, and 'the freezing horror of the treason sweeps from the Ford's theatre audience to the real audience beyond the screen'. This is a fear that produces yet more fear, a suggestion that multiplies when, at least for a moment, the 'real crowd touched with terror beholds its

244 Karl Marx, *Economic and Philosophical Manuscripts of 1844* in Karl Marx and Friedrich Engels, *Collected Works, Volume 3: Karl Marx, March 1843–August 1844* (London: Lawrence & Wishart, 1975), p. 313 (translation modified).

245 Vachel Lindsay, *The Art of the Moving Picture* (New York: Macmillan, 1916[1915]), p. 47.

natural face in the glass'[246]—the unmistakable physiognomy of the compact mass which (above all and in every-
body else) dreads itself.

50. '[L]anguage [ . . . ] only arises from the need, the
necessity of intercourse with other men.'[247] This birth is
continuous and pushes languages to their edges, forcing
the word to clash with the sign while referring both back
to the gesture.

This is also why—as Adorno and Ursula Jaerisch
explained—'social theory and physiognomy merge'.
When a dispute over wages, which is 'still always, potentially, a class struggle', is kept on the hither side of struggle 'by the integrated organizations that partake in the
power to control'; and when, once they've carried out
their crassest function, these organizations leave behind
a fine, diffuse and internalized shadow in the mass of
individuals busy finding work within work while their
unemployed and surplus peers compress them, it is then
that 'things cannot go smoothly'.[248]

No longer just in particular groups but in the
entire controlled mass, conflict explodes in a deformed
guise. Here 'envy, litigiousness, induced aggressiveness
deflected from its true object, these old inheritances of
the petty bourgeoisie' reappear 'with the greatest tenac-
ity'. And as always, 'they constitute a dangerous potential

246 Ibid., p. 49.

247 Karl Marx and Friedrich Engels, *The German Ideology* in
*Collected Works, Volume 5: Marx and Engels, 1845–1847* (London:
Lawrence & Wishart, 1976), p. 44.

248 Theodor W. Adorno and Ursula Jaerisch, 'Anmerkungen zum
sozialen Konflikt heute' [Notes on Social Conflict Today] (1968)
in *Soziologische Schriften*, I (Rolf Tiedemann ed.) (Frankfurt:
Suhrkamp, 1972), p. 188.

ANDREA CAVALLETTI | 130

not so much from the standpoint of order but for detested minorities or for those who are not politically conformist.'[249]

But a caesura is nonetheless possible. In fact, 'even pseudo-private conflicts are mediated by the social objectivity of language'.[250] Therefore, language itself knows of a different tonality, which at times stands out in the starkest way. If explosive spite both does not discern and hides the mediations from whence it comes, if it thrashes about amid social relationships as in a world of inert things, bumping into invisible hierarchies as if against thick domestic walls, it is instead in a slightly different, fleeting tonality—whereby language still arises from need and for which need transforms itself into language—that mediacy itself comes to expression.

This tonality is called *lament*. In it, and only in it, does there appear the gesture, face or voice of the struggling class. And it cannot vanish, not even when control replaces simple contrapositions with a modulation of contrasts, while it scatters, dilates and interposes its spectrum of a hundred greys; it cannot vanish *since it is fleetingness itself*. In the words of Gershom Scholem, '[l]ament is the only possible [ . . . ] volatile [*labile*] language.'[251] Lament—class struggle—does not lose itself in the continuous fluctuation of social relations because '[t]here is no stability of lament'.[252] Lament therefore escapes ritual and does not fix and extinguish itself in

249 Ibid.

250 Ibid., p. 190.

251 Gershom Scholem, 'On Lament and Lamentation' (1917–1918) (Lina Barouch and Paula Schwebel trans), *Jewish Studies Quarterly* 21(1) (2014): 7.

252 Ibid.

lamentation; it remains alive and resounds in love as in those tendencies that are called 'confidence, courage, humor, cunning, and fortitude'.[253] These resources, which seem so rare and limited in their effects, enjoy the highest political import. The separation of public from private, of the political from the unpolitical, is in fact mythical and operates, in the unlimited society, by occluding and enabling the manifestations of the crowd, even in the most restricted contexts. But lament penetrates every sphere and its absence reveals the class enemy even in the words of the neighbour. The most vivid tendencies of lamentation in fact constantly 'come back to the apparently accomplished in order to begin it afresh'.[254] Thus, they 'constantly call into question every victory, past and present, of the rulers'.[255]

51. In one of the preparatory notes for his theses (Ms 1098 r), Benjamin questions 'the removal of every echo of the "lament" from history' (*die Beseitigung jedes Nachhalls der «Klage» aus der Geschichte*). We owe to the philological genius of Arsène Darmesteter the restitution of the two *selichot*, the elegies—one written in Hebrew, the other in French vernacular (but still in Hebrew script)—for the auto-da-fé of Troyes of 24 April 1288, when 13 Jews were targets of the blood libel and burnt at the stake by order of the Inquisition. Darmesteter demonstrated that the elegies were penned by a single author (Rabbi Jacob bar Juda, who lived in Lorraine at the end of the thirteenth century). He also showed that the French *selichah* is not, as one might have

---

253 Benjamin, 'On the Concept of History', p. 390.

254 Marx, 'The Eighteenth Brumaire', p. 106.

255 Benjamin, 'On the Concept of History', p. 390.

thought, a slavish translation of the Hebraic text, but 'on the contrary, dominates it'.[256] Though both texts register the impressions of an eyewitness, the one in Hebrew, which composes biblical verses in the form of a cento, seems rather artificial, while the other is 'freer, clearer and more precise';[257] it is also richer in details: the 14th strophe, for example, reports a detail about the Dominican monks who visited Isaac Cohen, expecting him to abjure, on pain of the death penalty; and it testifies to Isaac's refusal and sacrifice. Thus, while the Hebrew testament testifies that Isaac Châtelain died on the Shabbat, the other affirms he was a rich man and a talented author. On the one hand, we have the rhetorical richness of the symbolism (the just man dies on Saturday, a pure life ends on the day of purity), on the other, the documentary sobriety of observation (Isaac was well off, a writer; they killed him and his family). These differences, as Darmesteter glosses following Ernest Renan, 'make evident the superiority of popular language over the language of doctors, when it comes to expressing an authentic sentiment'.[258] And if the Hebrew text really is chronologically prior (as a note in the ancient manuscript affirms), then the translation would have filled a lack in the original, elevating it, through the simplicity of dialect, to the true life of lament. For the linguistic order of observation [*constatazione*] is alone in not betraying or removing the fruit of injustice and violence; only in it do the unheeded word and unexpressed pain

256 Arsène Darmesteter, 'L'Autodafé de Troyes (24 avril 1288)', *Revue des Études Juives* 64 (1881): 219.

257 Ibid.

258 Ibid.: 218–20. See Arsène Darmesteter, 'Deux Élégies du Vatican', *Romania* 3 (1874): 484.

have a voice.[259] Therefore, true laments are always testimonies, unbound, however, from juridical claims. This is the case for the magnificent elegy *Telunah al ha-zeman* (Lament on Time, or on Destiny, *c*.1503) regarding the persecuted life of Judah Abrabanel. The tenor of truth here does not stem from any solemn and binding declarations but from the first observation, the soberest, which attains the letter of the *Book of Job* (30:31), since it says what it cannot not say, the mutation of language itself: 'I scorn song; I already broke my lute, / and hung my harp to the willows; / I have turned my song into loud laments / my flute vibrates with a ghostly tone within my sorrow.'[260]

Kafka insisted on the impossibility of translating Yiddish into German: it can be rendered in French—this did not seem too difficult—but if it is translated into German, it disappears, leaving in its place something inanimate. The relationship between the two languages is too delicate and meaningful to withstand translation. The examples that Kafka chooses to illustrate this relation are also meaningful and eloquent: '*Toit*, for instance, is not the same thing as *tot* (dead) and *blüt* is far from being

259 Milner has shown how in a Greek fragment reconstructed by Emile Benveniste from a Homeric cast, the introduction of a 'we' (*hémeas*) answers to this demand originating in a language that speaks '*sur le mode du constat et non pas de la persuasion*', in the modality of observation rather than persuasion. Here the 'we of the linguist who invents *hémeas* becomes . . . a "we" of the collective rather than an authorial we' (Jean-Claude Milner, *Le Périple structural. Figures et paradigm* [Larasse: Verdier, 2008(2002)], p. 106).

260 Judah Abrabanel (Leo Hebraeus), 'Telunah al ha-zeman' (*c*.1503) in *Mivhar ha-Shirah ha-Ivrit be-Italyah* (Jefim Hayyim Schirmann ed.) (Berlin: Schocken, 1934), pp. 216–22; Italian translation: 'Lamento sopra il destino' in *Dialoghi d'amore* (Santino Caramella ed.) (Bari: Laterza, 1929), p. 399.

*blut* (blood)'.[261] No other words are needed for the most elusive proximity to reveal its nature. Yiddish is a German that in small accents, faint songs, whistles and aspirated letters has begun to lament or, rather, has become a lament from beginning to end. Thus, Medium and High German forms survive in it; linguistic fragments seemingly on the brink of extinction do not cease to echo in the continuous ferment of popular speech. As Kafka says, what has entered the ghetto does not leave it so easily. A German version would therefore be fatal: Yiddish can never go back to that from whence it came; to turn German again as though nothing had ever happened—because that 'nothing' is Yiddish itself. On this impossibility of translation converge the histories of language, persecution and assimilation, the history of Judaism and the impossibility of a German Jewish world. In this vertigo, images of Troyes reappear vividly. It is for this selfsame reason that the story of the auto-da-fé is safeguarded in a particular version of the *selichah*, the one in the idiom shared with the executioners, which, like the German within the Yiddish, here becomes nothing but lament, from strophe to strophe.

The revolutionary class does not impose itself through a violent partition; it is instead violence that divides and separates a class of the oppressed. But in doing so, it also separates and frees up a new sphere of language. *I can't speak the sounds that show no pain . . .* The one who truly laments does not have any power to do so; rather, it is impossible for him not to lament. Yes,

---

261 Franz Kafka, 'An Introductory Talk on the Yiddish Language' in Mark M. Anderson (ed.), *Reading Kafka: Prague, Politics and the Fin de Siècle* (New York: Schocken, 1989), p. 266.

the 'lamenting pack' described by Canetti[262] is still, with its ambivalent character, simply a crowd; a crowd that comes together for the sake of lamentation, in the anguish and excited affirmation that, faced with death, something remains possible—namely, to unite in a throng, to grieve around the dying only then to flee, still united by the terror of the dead. But true lament is not a cry or lamentation, nor a mass ritual; it does not resonate with the obsessive rhythms of the assembly, it lives in loosening. It is not the desperate affirmation that something is possible in spite of it all, because within it we find the ultimate privation, impossibility itself becoming language. That is why, in the words of Kafka, lament 'can stand up to this fear'.[263] And it does not retreat. Even when everything is done to reduce it to the old ranks or sounds—with zealous, useless and stifled voices.

52. As soon as lament wells up in the revolutionary guide, he loses himself in the lament of the hundreds of thousands. This is why lament can belong to the group or the individual but it does not allow either the group or the individual to remain at once isolated and compressed; it temporally reunites them with the class, which now both appears and extends itself within them, even where it seems unable to recollect itself. From the outside, therefore, the actions and resources of lament can seem irrational, meagre, mad—only then to appear, all of a sudden, as real and truly threatening. This is because lamenting actions are not ineffective, nor mad or desperate, but completely exempt from opportunism. Whence their singular force which frees them from antagonisms

262 Canetti, *Crowds and Power*, pp. 103–7.
263 Kafka, 'An Introductory Talk on the Yiddish Language', p. 266.

and immediate interests. Lament, which turns to humour in the worker's speech (Marx), is not to be found in the false courage and songs of those pacifists described by Anders, but as 'a drastic, not infertile expression' of impossibility;[264] it echoes in the words of Benjamin to Scholem as well as in the silent mass of the deported of whom Bettelheim speaks. In the midst of the concentration camp, they tell themselves 'not even the Gestapo can kill us all'. And this is true, contrary to all expectations. For in the time of lament, they are many, many more than those gathered in the square; for they are now so compacted in that space as to grow and form a single mass, at once loosened and in solidarity. This is the class of the oppressed, the revolutionary class, which even the most solitary individual joins when he truly begins lamenting and finally stops being afraid.

In the end, even Isaac Babel fell into lament, in rather strange and variable ways. Hearing those groans, Antonina Nikolaevna Pirožkova hurried to her lover's room; he continued for a while longer, and bursting into a laugh, would say: 'I have just been demonstrating for you "the Jewish lament".'[265] Babel was well aware that in relation to the agonies and cries of the individual, the true and thus imperceptible lament is but a smile. This lament is in fact turned towards pleasure while pleasure is affirmed and maintained in the extinguishing of the lament. In the same way, in the revolutionary class, in solidarity itself, there are no obligations, nothing and nobody is solid. Where lament is in solidarity with pleasure, there is no law.

264 Benjamin and Scholem, *Correspondence*, p. 110.

265 A. N. Pirozhkova, *At His Side: The Last Years of Isaac Babel* (Anne Frydman and Robert L. Busch trans) (South Royalton, VT: Steerforth Press, 1996), p. 98 (translation modified).

**53.** 'Class' has been a biopolitical term; and in this sense a French invention. Introduced into the vocabulary of the art of government by the physiocrats, in their system it has a precise and irrevocable function: it is the concept thanks to which the phenomenon of 'population' becomes intelligible as a natural phenomenon, that is, in words of Foucault from his 1977–78 course: 'accessible to agents and techniques of transformation [that] are at once enlightened, reflected, analytical, calculated, and calculating'.[266] And if it is precisely through this naturalness that biopower can organize itself, that every political economy can calibrate itself, it is because in the texts of the physiocrats, class carries out an essential mediation: it establishes the link between society and nature, organizing an internally coherent system of social life that also conforms to the natural order. This has been ably demonstrated by Marie-France Piguet.[267] We should simply add that with this physiocratic innovation, there also enters the scene for the first time a certain dynamism, an instability to which we are now entirely accustomed. Classification is essential if population is to appear as an effective concept, but the government of population— namely, the attainment of its most convenient equilibrium—implies a continuous and gradual process. It will thus be supplemented with the completely new name of *civilization*. This is no derivative but recalls in turn the division into classes—the relationship is one of mutual implication.

266 Michel Foucault, *Security, Territory, Population: Lectures at the Collège de France, 1977–78* (Michel Senellart ed., Graham Burchell trans.) (London: Palgrave Macmillan, 2009), p. 71.

267 Marie-France Piguet, *Classe. Histoire du mot et genèse du concept des Physiocrates aux Historiens de la Restauration* (Lyon: Presses Universitaires de Lyon, 1966).

When the authors of the Restoration instead placed the term 'class' in the domain of history, when—following Saint-Simon (again according to Piguet)—they introduced the syntagm 'class struggle', they certainly linked the very idea of modern history to that of antagonism, to the deep, tangible division of the social and political body. But in so doing, the distance they took from the physiocratic paradigm only served to make it more powerful. As a lecture by François Guizot recites:

> [T]he struggle, instead of rendering society stationary, has been a principal cause of its progress; the relations of the different classes with one another; the necessity of combating and of yielding by turns; the variety of interests [ . . . ] from all this has probably sprung the most energetic, the most productive principle of development in European civilization. This struggle of the classes has been constant; enmity has grown up between them [ . . . ] yet they have progressively approached, assimilated, and understood each other.[268]

You don't need to be a good Leninist to recall Marx's letter to Weydemeyer of 5 March 1852: 'Now as for myself, I do not claim to have discovered either the existence of classes in modern society or the struggle between them. Long before me, bourgeois historians [ . . . ]'.[269] We know that Marx read Guizot. And against the latter's idea of civilization and progress, as much as

---

268 François Pierre Guillaume Guizot, *General History of Civilization in Europe* (George Wells Knight ed.) (New York: D. Appleton & Company, 1896[1828]), pp. 206–7.

269 Karl Marx, 'Letter to Joseph Weydemeyer' (5 March 1852) in Karl Marx and Friedrich Engels, *Collected Works, Volume 39: Letters, 1852–1855* (London: Lawrence & Wishart, 1983), p. 62.

against Proudhon's apologia for the coup d'état, he showed as a historian 'how the *class struggle* in France created circumstances and relations that made it possible for a grotesque mediocrity to play a hero's part'.[270] In Marx, the *new use* of the syntagm 'class struggle' disarms the theory of civilization, breaks the double bind and exits the biopolitical horizon. Without forgetting *State and Revolution*, let us reread the second part of that famous passage:

> [B]ourgeois historians had described the historical development of this struggle between the classes, as had bourgeois economists their economic anatomy. My own contribution was 1. to show that the *existence of classes* is merely bound up with *certain historical phases in the development of production*; 2. That the class struggle necessarily leads to the *dictatorship of the proletariat*; 3. that this dictatorship itself constitutes no more than a transition to the *abolition of all classes* and to a *classless society*.[271]

Being against Guizot also means being against bourgeois economists. We can thus argue, by way of summary, that there is something in this new idea of class struggle that does not conform to the horizon of political economy, just as it does not fit in that of bourgeois historiography, in the standpoint of civilization. That something is effective solidarity. And if Marx understands the latter as struggle or true civil war, if it is only in solidarity that association acquires a political character. Effective

---

270 Karl Marx, 'Preface to the Second Edition of the *Eighteenth Brumaire of Napoleon Bonaparte*' in Karl Marx and Friedrich Engels, *Collected Works, Volume 21: Marx and Engels, 1867–1870* (London: Lawrence & Wishart, 1986), p. 57.

271 Marx, 'Letter to Joseph Weydemeyer' (5 March 1852), pp. 62–5.

solidarity is also the internal movement that abolishes all antagonisms and thus every political division. If, as the result of struggle, classless society can replace its bourgeois counterpart, it is because it is already present in the medium of struggle itself. Whence the definition (in the *Critique of the Gotha Programme*, 1875) of the dictatorship of the proletariat as a 'political transition period' (*politische Übergangsperiode*). What is political—that is, in Marx's terms, what still corresponds to antagonisms—is precisely the character that the union of workers in struggle takes on from an external and exclusive point of view, as long as that point of view survives. As long as and everywhere that one of the *dispositifs* called mediation, employment or unemployment, labour organization or free time is still operative, classless society will only be a dictatorship of the proletariat.

**54.** Jean-Claude Milner has outlined the latest evolution of the bourgeoisie or, better, the passage from the still Proustian bourgeoisie of rent and property to the new waged bourgeoisie. What distinguishes and decrees the triumph of the latter is a wage that, unlike the proletarian one, no longer depends on the minimal price of labour-power. Moreover, its price is arbitrary, entirely 'political' and systematically higher than any economic rationale would warrant. Where there is a bourgeoisie, there operates the *dispositif* of the surplus-wage (*sursalaire*), that Milner registers in its two alternative facets as *surrémunération* (surplus-remuneration) and *surtemps* (surplus-time, qua free time after work).[272]

In the classical scheme (as in Benjamin), the waged bourgeoisie was the clerical stratum (which obviously

272 Milner, *Le Salaire de l'idéal.*

formed, alongside artisans and other consumers, a part of the petty bourgeoisie). We cannot simply say that the whole stage is now occupied by clerical workers. Milner is not describing a sociological advance; he brings to light a structural mutation. But it is still within the new waged bourgeoisie that there exists and is constantly being formed a compressed petty bourgeoisie—as ferocious as its precursor. Only that its ferocity does not necessarily refer back to the ghosts of 1929—it is not an effect of bankruptcy or a presage of the great crisis. As is evident today, the new petty bourgeoisie shows it is capable of anything when it risks losing that which defines it as such: the *surplus* of its salary and time. It becomes racist with ease when a little free time or bonus money are at stake. Its ferocity is the ferocity of leisure. And the hypocrisy to which it happily resorts, according to which in the end it is the weakest and the most exploited (our poor working-class men) who suffer the presence of the still weaker and more exploited (immigrants), is not merely vacuous and deranged. It contains the formula for including the proletariat into the compacted mass— a formula that was already useful at the origins of fascism and is so widespread today, in vivid projections of fears and desires. The result of this strategy is well known: diffuse discretionary powers, hordes of policemen, all kinds of violence (always justified), only apparently arbitrary acts which are ultimately grounded in the iron law of social recreation, on the protection of leisure or, better, on its definitive formula: for this will always be nothing more than 'periodic and regulated [leisure], considered a duty among the most sacred and not a mere pleasure'.[273]

273 Gabriel Tarde, *Psychologie économique, Tome I* (Paris: Félix Alcan, 1902), p. 120.

—O holy, just rest, gazing upon the holiness of labour, O, to devote oneself to your cult wholeheartedly, to be its minister, or at least its mayor! . . . and let's leaf through the cruel catalogue of weekend passions.

Benjamin described the opposite movement. He recognized the formation of a non-class as the most dangerous outcome of all class antagonisms, the quintessence of all tensions, ready to reproduce itself everywhere and without exceptions, in the guise of an unlimited or 'planetary petty bourgeoisie'.[274] Benjamin's idea of a society without crowds is therefore the perfect complement to Marx's vision. For the power of solidarity is not just beyond the grasp of the old economists who think in terms of the theory of mere interest, of *Homo oeconomicus* shuttered in his own egoisms, but also of those critical voices in economic psychology who, basing themselves on the only seemingly heterogeneous concepts of prestige, influence, faith, etc., do not depart from Tarde's position. For the latter, the general strike—solidarity irreducible to the mere logic of interest or to the laws of desires and beliefs—could not but appear as a collective hallucination, a phenomenon of the most vivid and uncontrollable fanaticism.

The word 'society' now names the unlimited rule of antagonisms and suggestions: foci of attraction, leaders and ranks, great flows or small imitative vortices, more or less intensified tensions. In other words, we are always dealing with the petty bourgeoisie, with its elemental drives, its desire to prevail, the bitterness and fear compounded in the myth of security.

---

274 Giorgio Agamben, *The Coming Community* (Michael Hardt trans.) (Minneapolis: University of Minnesota Press, 1993), p. 62.

In Benjamin, the word 'solidarity' names the anti-psychological act that dissolves the crowd. He thus conferred a new meaning to 'what communist tacticians call "winning over the petty bourgeoisie"'—as the 1936 note recites.[275] This is not a work of proselytism; it is not about persuading anybody, especially not the instinctual mass, ready for anything, no longer persuadable due to its excess of credulity. It is a matter of avoiding its formation. Today, confronted with new pogroms and state racisms, the 'winning over' cannot be undertaken in any other way—only through true solidarity, which upends the compact mass, transforming it into a revolutionary class, that is to say, from crowd simply into class.

55. Yes, the word 'class' was pronounced at the dawn biopower in order to affirm the reasons of landowners in the jargon of the *économistes*. In the current phase, it is the business enterprise that lays down the law and the state that coincides with the enterprise—or with the enterprise's smokescreen. Everywhere, instinctive stupidity rules, the kind unleashed by the manager. The latter lives—as Hermann Broch could still argue—in an entirely characteristic 'state of suggestion', a 'semiconscious' or 'twilight' state (*Dämmerzustand*). By identifying himself completely with interest, the manager shuts himself up in a world of mere concreteness from which ideas are banished and where satisfaction for every victory is inseparable from the (basically homicidal) satisfaction for the defeat (and ultimately death) of the adversary. His stupefaction, his 'twilight being' (*Dämmerwesen*) thus extends into 'the play of a magical-sadistic structure'

275 Benjamin, 'The Work of Art', p. 129.

(*magisch-sadistische Spielstruktur*)[276] that penetrates and shapes society as a whole.

Thus, if the condition of intensified antagonism appears completely natural (one is born into a corporation and always already thrown into its beguiling projects), the word 'class' should now simply disappear, and naturally so. It should disappear, when the worst of the world can become obvious and—in gestures, words, physiognomies—all of its grotesqueness ordinary.

Yes, there no longer seems to be any margin keeping apart state, society and enterprise. This is because (as Foucault taught us) the enterprise was never simply an institution but was also from the start a political technique, a way of acting in the economic field, a social function. This is the spell of limitless sadism: the enterprise effectively enacts (also through the state apparatus) the unlimited inclusion into the entrepreneurial society.

Instead it is precisely in the face of this latest superpower and violence that the name 'class' cannot fail to resound, even if it is with the most ephemeral accent, in the most minimal observation.

## Benjaminian Coda

The ideas that make up a consistent thought do not at first emerge as mere sketches; only later, as the years go by, they do so in the guise of clearer and more mature arguments. They make their appearance in an already accomplished albeit contracted form, and then in new,

276 Hermann Broch, *Massenwahntheorie: Beiträge zu einer Psychologie der Politik* in *Kommentierte Werkausgabe, XII* (Paul Michael Lützeler ed.) (Frankfurt: Suhrkamp, 1979), pp. 159–60.

slightly altered abbreviations. A terminological correspondence can sometimes allow them to be recognized.

In its manifest sociological meaning, the term
*Auflockerung* ('loosening') expresses an alteration in the
cohesion of an expanding group. As Simmel says in the
foundational text of urban sociology, 'The Metropolis and
Mental Life' (1903): 'To the extent to which the group
grows [ . . . ] to the same degree the group's direct, inner
unity loosens (*lockert sich*), and the rigidity of the original
demarcations against others is softened through mutual
relations and connections.'[277] In Benjamin's 1936 note
on class, this meaning takes on a new and original tonality. In fact, *Auflockerung* belongs fully to the Benjaminian
laboratory, appearing several times, before and after the
'36 note, in writings that are in many respects close
to 'The Work of Art in the Age of Its Technological
Reproducibility'. In the two versions (1931 and 1939) of
the important text on the work of Bertolt Brecht, 'What
Is Epic Theatre?', 'loosening' designates both the condition of the audience and the technique employed by the
director. As Benjamin explains, like the dance instructor
with his young pupil, the director who stages a historic
event tries, first and foremost, to unknot and loosen
(*auflockern*) the articulations of the plot, disregarding the
important choices and decisions that the audience
expects and shining the spotlight instead on 'the incom-
mensurable and the singular'.[278] We are dealing with that
process of 'literalization' of the theatre by means of plac-
ards and captions through which Brecht withdraws the
dimension of sensation from events. While dramatic

277 Simmel, 'The Metropolis and Mental Life', p. 180.
278 Benjamin, 'What Is Epic Theatre? [First Version]', in *Understanding Brecht* (Anna Bostock trans.) (London: Verso, 1998), p. 8.

sequences produce 'a collection of hypnotized test subjects'[279] who react docilely in the grip of an ancient habit
(to reprise another famous Benjaminian *topos*, what is
the tradition of the victors if not a training in suggestion?), epic theatre interrupts the momentum of events
and exposes the singular situation, which thus lends
itself to detached analysis. Brecht said that in the old dramatic theatre, 'suggestion is used', while in the epic one,
'arguments are used'.[280] To use Benjamin's terms, the
plot's *Auflockerung* (or even its '*epische Streckung*', its epic
dilatation or stretching) is at the same time the loosening
of the audience; now, 'the false and deceptive totality
called "audience"'—that is to say, the 'mass as such', the
'compact mass' (as the 'men of Mahagonny' will be
defined in 1939, in the 'Commentaries to Some Poems
by Brecht')—'begins to disintegrate and there is new
space for the formation of separate parties within it—
separate parties corresponding to conditions as they
really are.'[281] Brechtian technique is in effect the experimental paradigm for revolutionary action: it's an anti-
suggestive didactics or exercise that counters the
continuous production of a reactive audience with the
transformation of spectators themselves into 'collabora-
tors'. As Benjamin says in his 1934 Paris lecture, 'The
Author as Producer':

> The purpose of epic theatre is to construct out
> of the smallest elements of behaviour what

279 Ibid., p. 2.

280 Bertolt Brecht, 'Notes on the Opera *Rise and Fall of the City of
Mahagonny*' (1936) in *Brecht on Theatre*, 3rd EDN (Marc Silberman,
Steve Giles and Tom Kuhn eds) (London: Bloomsbury, 2015), p. 111.

281 Benjamin, 'What Is Epic Theatre?', p. 10; 'Commentaries on
Poems by Brecht' in *Understanding Brecht* (Anna Bostock trans.)
(London: Verso, 1998), p. 48.

Aristotelian drama calls 'action'. Its means, therefore, are more modest than those of traditional theatre; its aims likewise. It sets out, not so much to fill the audience with feelings—albeit possibly feelings of revolt—as to alienate the audience in a lasting manner, through thought, from the conditions in which it lives.[282]

Only in loosening does the thinking of the mass—we can now say taking up the 1936 note again—'[cease] to be governed by mere reactions; it makes the transition to action.'[283]

It is now time to clarify what could seem obvious: namely, the expression 'separate parties corresponding to conditions as they really are'. This constitutes a canonical definition of the antagonistic class. But is loosening really reducible to this?

The answer is, so to speak, in a philological register. In those years, Benjamin was reprising, from a political perspective, a technical term from his reflections on aesthetics. The 1914–15 essay, 'Two Poems by Friedrich Hölderlin', distinguishes between the ideal that inspires the poet: namely, the 'poetized' (*Gedichtete*), and the form that the poet has been able to confer to it, that is, the poem (*Gedicht*) as the poetized's actual albeit limited determination. Something in the poetized remains potential, and it's up to the good exegete to address it. How can he do it? Has this not become a distant ideal, a vague and ineffable shadow? To the contrary, as Benjamin underscores, it stands out 'solely through its greater determinability; not through a quantitative lack

---

282 Walter Benjamin, 'The Author as Producer' in *Understanding Brecht*, (Anna Bostock trans.) (London: Verso, 1998), p. 100–1.

283 Benjamin, 'The Work of Art', p. 129.

of determinations but through the potential existence of those that are effectively [*aktuell*] present in the poem—and others'.[284]

There follows a definition that is essential to our argument: 'The poetized (*Gedichtete*) is a loosening up of the firm functional coherence that reigns in the poem (*Gedicht*) itself.'[285] The exegesis forces the textual datum, bends its joints, loosens or stretches its prosodic ties and, disregarding some obvious links, lets appear 'a variety of possibilities of connection'.[286] It thereby undertakes the 'ever stricter determination' or 'higher degree of determination' of the poetized.[287]

Here, then, the political definition of *Auflockerung* is also illuminated. We can say that the revolutionary class is not something vague by contrast with the mass that is more or less compressed by its biopolitical ties (according to the ever shifting but always selfsame mythologies of nation, soil, blood, race and *Volk*). Because it is indeed a 'separate party', corresponding to the real divisions that structure the social, class is not reducible to them. When internally loosened, it becomes the potential existence of the actual determinations of society, *and of others*. This is how we need to understand the phrase from 1936: 'loosening [ . . . ] is the work of solidarity'.[288] No longer riveted to their situation but

284 Walter Benjamin, 'Two Poems by Friedrich Hölderlin' in *Selected Writings, Volume 1, 1913–1926* (Marcus Bullock and Michael W. Jennings eds) (Cambridge, MA: Harvard University Press, 1996), p. 19.

285 Ibid.

286 Ibid.

287 Ibid.

288 Benjamin, 'The Work of Art', p. 129.

enduringly estranged, beings remain always determinable, capable of unprecedented behaviours, that is to say, of all possibilities of connection.

## *Class against Class*

ALBERTO TOSCANO

> Other classes, having come to power, protect
> what they got
> While dictating to everybody else the novel way
> of getting.
> This class conquers the goods-producing
> works by wholly repealing
> The way they are got. This class has nothing to
> safeguard for itself.
> To the contrary, any individual safeguard it has
> to destroy.
>
> Bertolt Brecht,
> 'The Manifesto' (1945)
> (Darko Suvin trans.)

The spectre of class haunts our present, but in ways no communist would deem fit to celebrate. Long after the cynical grandchildren of the Second International promoted the euthanasia of social antagonism in favour of glittering vistas of financialized affluence, and myriad farewells to the proletariat were sung in the halls of academia, that apparent industrial anachronism, the working class, has made a grotesque, spectacular return. National, male, white, this is a class whose discursive

prominence is proportional to the ambiguity of its refer-
ent. Propped up by dubious marketing categories—such
as those that divide the British body politic into ABC1 and
C2DE—it is a potent fantasy of (threatened) identity
and belonging, emphatically not a relation to the apparatuses of production, exploitation and accumulation
(which would reveal a proletariat neither predominantly
national, nor male, nor white). Labour and production
have returned as objects of nostalgic *ressentiment*: the
superstructure as a dream of the base. Far from consti-
tuting a betrayal of an unsullied history of conflict and
emancipation, the reactionary trope of the abandoned
working class is a legacy of the capture, integration and
promotion of class as a crucial operator in the workings
of the national-social state, whose reality and representa-
tion continues to shape and constrain our present.[1] It is
not simply that, as Marx famously avowed and Cavalletti
reminds us, class was a product of bourgeois historiography and political economy; a defence of the working
class can very well be articulated in exclusionary and reactionary terms, which are not properly accounted for by the
idea of the 'betrayal' of a naturally progressive impulse.
The contradictory, internally antagonistic history of the
working class is not just a story of solidarity against the
odds, triumphs of discipline, Sisyphean efforts to civilize
capital and epic insurgencies to terminate it; it is also a
record of 'hate strikes' for racially exclusive trade unions,
passionate attachments to empire, chauvinism bolstered
by ideologies of labour, anti-immigrant demands for a
national preference in the labour market, fascism taking

1 See Étienne Balibar, 'The Nation Form: History and Ideology' in
Étienne Balibar and Immanuel Wallerstein, *Race, Nation, Class:
Ambiguous Identities* (Chris Turner trans. [for Étienne Balibar])
(London: Verso, 1988), pp. 86–106.

on the mantle of the 'proletarian nation'. It is the latter history that we find indicted in Lenin's fulminations against social imperialism and the labour aristocracy, in DuBois' enduring diagnosis of the psychological wages of whiteness, in radical and Third World feminisms agitating for wages for housework and revealing the intimate bonds between patriarchy, racism and capital.

In other words, class is not just a name for social and political division; it must itself be divided, its historical fault lines traced, its ethical ruptures identified. It is to this project of dividing class that Cavalletti has made a vital contribution. First, he has placed class within a history of our present that connects it, following Foucault, to the emergence of biopolitical modes of government, but also relates it to an intense theoretical debate—straddling psychology, sociology, philosophy and literature—on mass psychology and techniques of suggestion, one which remains profoundly relevant to our conjuncture. Second, he has developed a profound if somewhat peripheral intuition of Walter Benjamin to explore the ways in which a politics of class can sever the latter's ties to biopolitical myths of security, the manipulability of crowds and the ordering of capitalist society, engendering an image of solidarity that repels the lures of identity and renders itself impervious to the techniques of mass suggestion.

We have grown accustomed to thinking of class as a concept not just distinct from but in a sense antithetical to those of mass, crowd or population. From the vantage point of Cavalletti's archaeological endeavour, we can recognize instead the profound ties that bind it to these other figures of the collective. Cavalletti follows these threads through a creative appropriation and reorientation of the notion of the biopolitical. The latter was centrally at stake in his first book—*La città biopolitica. Mitologie della sicurezza* [The Biopolitical City: Mythologies of Security][2]—in which Foucault and Agamben's historical and philosophical insights[3] are expanded upon to provide a fascinating reconstruction of urbanism as a key biopolitical science and an analysis of spatialization as a decisive dynamic in the politics of populations. By contrast with an anglophone reception that (over-)emphasizes Foucault's analyses of neoliberalism in a periodizing direction, and in which the very notion of governmentality has been understood as a tool for grasping (or even promoting) the overcoming of class politics, Cavalletti presents class as inextricable from biopolitics and vice versa. As he writes in this book:

> 'Class' has been a biopolitical term; and in this sense a French invention. Introduced into the vocabulary of the art of government by the physiocrats, in their system it has a precise and irrevocable function: it is the concept thanks to which the phenomenon of 'population' becomes intelligible as a natural phenomenon, that is, in words of Foucault from his 1977–78 course: 'accessible to agents and techniques of transformation [that] are at once enlightened, reflected, analytical, calculated, and calculating'. And if it is precisely through this naturalness that biopower can organize itself, that every political economy can calibrate itself, it is because in the texts of the physiocrats, class carries out an

2 Andrea Cavalletti, *La città biopolitica. Mitologie della sicurezza* (Milan: Bruno Mondadori, 2005).

3 Cavalletti, an erstwhile student of Agamben, has written illuminatingly on the ('an-archic') political core of the latter's *Homo Sacer* project in 'Usage et anarchie', *Critique* 836–7 (2017): 98–114.

essential mediation: it establishes the link between society and nature, organizing an internally coherent system of social life that also conforms to the natural order.[4]

This analysis dispatches the tendency to see class as a term that only attaches to disciplinary societies, with their 'accumulation of men', and which would thus be both peripheral to a biopolitics of populations and obsolete in contemporary societies of control. From the vantage point of Cavalletti's history of the present, from *Class* through *The Biopolitical City* and on to the third panel in a virtual triptych on the archaeology of contemporary power and counter-power—his essay on the history and psycho-politics of 'suggestion'[5]—this contrastive, periodizing use of the biopolitical does not obtain. Rather, in the political economy of the physiocrats, we see the inception of a line of thinking on class that will later intersect with the mass psychology of suggestion to shape a modern paradigm of power, in which 'class is there, between mass and suggestion, as an element of articulation, a kind of hinge'.[6] Mass, crowd, population and class are thus interwoven in a biopolitical process of 'civilization' and 'classification', at once material and imaginary, technical and spectacular; 'the appearance of the crowd,' as Cavalletti writes in a key passage, 'is internal to the suggestive spectacle of biopower.'[7] Governmentality is,

---

4 In this volume, p. 137.

5 Andrea Cavalletti, *Suggestione. Potenza e limiti del fascino politico* (Turin: Bollati Boringhieri, 2011). Themes in this book are further explored in Cavalletti's two forthcoming books, *Vertigo* and *The Inappropriable*.

6 Andrea Cavalletti, 'Massa, classe, suggestione' in *Attualità di Gabriel Tarde. Sociologia, Psicologia, Filosofia* (S. Prinzi ed.) (Naples: Orthotes, 2016), p. 109.

7 Ibid., p. 122.

contrary to received academic opinion, inseparable from 'an immense psycho-technical apparatus of mass sugges- tion'—an expression from Carl Schmitt that, according to Cavalletti, sought to grasp an illusory or theatrical dimension of the political that Marx had rigorously grasped through the notion that 'men and things become—in the society divided into classes—character masks (*Charaktermasken*) of power-relations'.[8] And far from merely standing for mutable multiplicities that transcend the demarcations and antagonisms of class, populations, beginning with the founding eighteenth- century text of biopolitical government, are always divided into true or false populations, normal and abnor- mal; they are profoundly polemical entities, even or espe- cially when their management is aimed at preventing the coming to political consciousness of antagonism.[9]

While Cavalletti's archaeological challenge to a pre- sentist and truncated notion of the biopolitical helpfully undercuts the tendency merely to juxtapose class and population, by indicating the source of both in bourgeois political economy, his articulation of the biopolitical with the late nineteenth-century debates on mass politics and mass suggestion is also an excellent antidote to a progres- sive temptation simply to invert the anti-socialist and anti-democratic condemnations of the crowd into its cel- ebration. To use a term from Károly Kerényi brilliantly deployed by Furio Jesi—the great mythologist, Germanist and political thinker whose work Cavalletti has been almost single-handedly responsible for recovering from studied neglect—the crowd or mass (the French *foule*, the German *Masse*, the Italian *folla* or *massa*) is also the effec- tive product of 'technicized myths' (especially of *ethnos*

8 Ibid., p. 120.

9 Ibid., p. 117; *La città biopolitica*, p. 66.

and nation), which cannot be dismissed as mere phantasmagorias.[10] Placing the crowd back into the 'fin de siècle nightmare'[11] from whence it sprang, in theory *and* reality, also means recognizing it as an actual if ambiguous product of political modernity, and requires that we think of class not merely as the other of the crowd but in intimate dialectic with it. In an essay on Hermann Broch's theory of mass madness that prolongs the arguments in *Class*, Cavalletti pointedly speaks of the 'still-relevant idea that politics must be a fight against the crowd'.[12] The continued influence of that tradition of the fear of the masses that courses through modern political thought and finds a potent late nineteenth-century crystallization in the writings of Gustave Le Bon—an influence palpable in recent dismissals and demonizations of the riot—should not distract us from acknowledging that, inasmuch as mass, crowd and population are real products of biopower. It is not just incumbent upon us to critique the theories of crowd pathology, we need to

10 For Cavalletti on Jesi, see his introductions to Furio Jesi, *Spartakus: The Symbology of Revolt* (Alberto Toscano trans.) (London: Seagull Books, 2013) and *Time and Festivity* (Cristina Viti trans.) (London: Seagull Books, forthcoming). Cavalletti's own method of inquiry, drawing among others from Foucault, Benjamin and Agamben, is also illuminated by his own comments on Jesi's approach to his literary and mythological materials. See Andrea Cavalletti, 'La maniera compositiva di Furio Jesi' in Furio Jesi, *Materiali mitologici. Mito e antropologia nella cultura mitteleuropea* (Andrea Cavalletti ed.), NEW EDN (Turin: Einaudi, 2001[1979]), pp. 359–76. In the same volume, Jesi had written of 'knowledge by composition: the choice and connection of images that [ . . . ] interacting with one another enacted an approximation to the figures'.

11 Cavalletti, 'Massa, classe, suggestione', p. 122.

12 Andrea Cavalletti, 'Peut-on soigner la folie des masses?', *Critique* 755 (2010): 341.

confront those pathological crowds themselves. That is because 'the crowd . . . this primary, *farouche* [savage], heterogeneous, instinctive being is both the *evil* and the *specific product* of the very same apparatus of classification of the social body'.[13] In the expression the 'fear of the crowd', we should thus discern both the objective and subjective genitive. Crowds are feared, crowds fear—other crowds, but also themselves. Elsewhere Cavalletti has noted that in 1936, the year of publication of Benjamin's essay on the work of art, whose note on class serves as the germ-cell for this book, Fritz Lang released his film *Fury*—in a crucial courtroom scene, the crowd who had tried to lynch the character played by Spencer Tracy sees its own actions projected on a screen and frightens itself.[14]

It is by unsettling the customary distinction between theories of class (consciousness) and theories of the (pathological) crowd that Walter Benjamin's footnote on class demonstrates its transformative potential. Chiming with, but innovating upon, the communist identification of the petty bourgeoisie as a key conduit for the politics of fascism, it operates a *détournement* of anti-socialist theories of the crowd to argue that it is not the proletariat, the lumpen, or the poor who make up the modern crowd, but a fearful, reactive, compact collective best captured in the figure of the petty bourgeoisie. As Cavalletti details, this intuition is further explored in Agamben's image of the planetary rise of the petty bourgeoisie as a post-his-

13 Cavalletti, 'Massa, classe, suggestione', p. 121.

14 'Il potere della folla. Quando le masse sono pericolose', Interview with Andrea Cavalletti, *La Repubblica*, 30 July 2009. It is not irrelevant to note the fact that Lang was obliged to centre his indictment of lynch law on a white character, thus displacing and partially occluding the profoundly racialized nature of crowd politics.

torical universal class, and Jean-Claude Milner's analysis of a new petty bourgeoisie always on the verge of racist rage when its leisure and privileges are under threat. In Benjamin's formulation:

> The mass [or crowd] as an impenetrable, compact entity, which Le Bon and others have made the subject of their 'mass psychology' is that of the petty bourgeoisie. The petty bourgeoisie is not a class; it is in fact only a mass. And the greater the pressure acting on it between the two antagonistic classes of the bourgeoisie and the proletariat, the more compact it becomes. In this mass, the emotional element described in mass psychology is indeed a determining factor. [ . . . ] Demonstrations by the compact mass thus always have a panicked quality—whether they give vent to war fever, hatred of Jews, or the instinct for self-preservation.[15]

And, in Cavalletti's incisive gloss:

> When there is no solidarity or consciousness, there is no class; there is only the petty-bourgeois mass, with its well-behaved psychology. [ . . . ] The petty bourgeoisie is not, as Benjamin teaches us, a class: it is only a compressed mass between the rich bourgeoisie and the proletariat. From this non-class, every fascism will produce its 'people', masking this mere compression in the archaic and inseparable names of community, fatherland, work, blood, leader.[16]

15 Quoted by Cavalletti in this volume, pp. 33–4.
16 In this volume, pp. 37, 55.

Through the prism of Cavalletti's commentary and montage, Benjamin's suggestion that class should be understood in terms of a *loosening* rather than a becoming compact, and that class solidarity is pitted against identity and belonging, corroborates Adorno's words in his otherwise sharply critical comments to his friend's work in progress on Baudelaire and the Paris Arcades: 'your few sentences about the disintegration of the proletariat as "masses" are among the profoundest and most powerful statements of political theory that I have encountered since I read [Lenin's] *State and Revolution.*'[17]

By placing Benjamin's incisive fragment in the context of his own archaeology of the biopolitical government of society, Cavalletti allows us to give this political theory its full scope, namely by conceiving of it as a way to dismantle biopolitics, thus continuing his earlier reflections on 'absolute defection'.[18] Rather than a positive or insurgent biopolitics, or an inversion of the multitude into a name for the political good, this Benjaminian politics is a revolutionary politics of class against the biopolitical management of class. Here Benjamin relays Marx's antivitalism. As Cavalletti notes, in Marx 'there is neither biologism nor hypostasis of life, not even in the guise of

---

17 Letter of 18 March 1936, sent from London, in Theodor W. Adorno, 'Letters to Walter Benjamin' in Ernst Bloch, Georg Lukács, Bertolt Brecht, Walter Benjamin, Theodor W. Adorno, *Aesthetics and Politics* (London: New Left Books, 1977), p. 126.

18 To quote the last lines of Cavalletti's first book: 'There is an anarchic possibility that does not confide—contrary to Schmitt's claims—in the natural goodness of man, nor does it recognize the oppositions between good and bad, political and apolitical; it does not presuppose war but changes the conditions of every conflict. From its vantage point, the opening and exposure to risk does not in fact differ from the supposed security or protection of biopolitics' (*La città biopolitica*, p. 249).

an original sharing, of being as being in common, of a sharing of life as such. Life as such is a myth, unlike solidarity.'[19]

It is worth fully appreciating the boldness of Cavalletti's move: what we have here is not a new valorization of the pathologized notions of mass or crowd; nor is it a return to the ultimately non-Marxian conviction of a convertibility between sociological classification and political agency; nor, finally, is it an effort philosophically to disjoin a pure, transcendental proletariat from an empirical working class.[20] Rather, it is an effort to think those political techniques and operations that could traverse and undo both the petty-bourgeois compact mass and the functional, biopolitical working class, for the

19 In this volume, p. 107.

20 In this regard, Cavalletti's approach, with its careful gleaning of the biopolitical and anti-biopolitical figures of class that mark what we could call the long nineteenth century, is more persuasive than Agamben's effort (in his otherwise striking articulation of Pauline *klēsis* and Marxian *Klasse*) simply to disjoin proletariat and working class, namely, when he declares that 'the fact that the proletariat ends up being identified over time with a determinate social class— the working class that claims prerogatives and rights for itself—is the worst misunderstanding of Marxian thought. What for Marx served as a strategic identification—the working class as *klēsis* and as historical figure contingent on the proletariat—becomes, to the opposite end, a true and proper substantial social identity that necessarily ends in losing its revolutionary vocation' (Giorgio Agamben, *The Time That Remains: A Commentary on the Letter to the Romans* [Patricia Daley trans.] [Stanford, CA: Stanford University Press, 2005], p. 31). Cavalletti also wishes to disarticulate class and social identity, but he does so, following Benjamin, from the viewpoint of a political praxis of this separation rather than on the basis of a distinction between a transcendental and an empirical class. Benjamin's revolutionary class is not contingently or extrinsically connected to the working class.

sake of new forms of revolutionary solidarity, to which Benjamin gave the enigmatic and evocative name of *loosening* (*Auflockerung*). It is in the light of this struggle against biopolitics, conceived as a synonym for capitalist political economy and power, that we can understand the claim that 'the "real civil war" cannot but be the dissolution of biopolitical borders themselves, a loosening of the interests on the basis of which even Deleuze and Guattari's slogan will allow itself to be overturned: *il y a toujours la carte variable de la classe sous la reproduction des masses*—beneath the reproduction of the masses there is always the variable map of class.'[21] This civil war is a *stásis* inside class, a way of dividing both its concept and its reality from the inside. Or, to put in a different way, class struggle is a struggle in and over class as well. As Cavalletti shows in his readings of Marx, as well as in his recovery of a fascinating figure on the margins of postwar Marxism, Jean Fallot—with his contrast between Epicurean pleasure and biopolitical desire—it is possible to articulate a decisive difference between class struggle as a mechanism for the regulation of life and production under capital (which is also to say for the compacting and compression of collectives and groups) and class struggle as a political and ethical experience of the dissolution of biopolitics.

Cavalletti's Marx is not the one who, as Foucault notoriously noted in *The Order of Things*, never leaves the epistemic element of nineteenth-century political economy; rather, his '*new use* of the syntagm "class struggle" disarms the theory of civilization, breaks the double bind and exits the biopolitical horizon.'[22] Rather than grounding politics in the existing structures and flows of

21 In this volume, p. 110.
22 In this volume, p. 139.

'society' as the transcendental object of modern biopolitics, class breaks (with) society, it exceeds it. Or, in Cavalletti's words: 'the revolutionary class is not something vague by contrast with the mass that is more or less compressed by its biopolitical ties (according to the ever shifting but always selfsame mythologies of nation, soil, blood, race and *Volk*). Because it is indeed a "separate party", corresponding to the real divisions that structure the social, class is not reducible to them.'[23] It this 'irreducible' figure of class, born of solidarity and hostile to any preconceived identity of race, nation or gender that transpires from Marx's observation in the 1844 *Manuscripts* on the solidarity of artisans: 'Association, society and conversation, which again has association as its end, are enough for them.'[24] It is also in this class, combatively loosening the bonds of crowd, mass and population, that we can recognize the sworn enemy of a politics of leadership, charisma or prestige, which is to say, a politics of suggestion. Its violence breaks with the 'violence of the aura'.[25] Understood in a non- or anti-biopolitical sense, class 'does not unite but, rather, separates mass and suggestion and does so by covering and eliminating prestige. Where there is no prestige, there is no mass suggestion, that is where we find class'.[26] Prestige, that aura of authority and device of suggestion

23 In this volume, p. 148.

24 Quoted in this volume, p. 128. On this passage in Marx, see also Antonia Birnbaum, 'Between Sharing and Antagonism: The Invention of Communism in the Early Marx', *Radical Philosophy* 166 (2011): 21–8.

25 *Die Gewalt des Nimbus*. This expression from Helmut Plessner is discussed by Cavalletti in 'Massa, classe, suggestione', pp. 112, 119.

26 'Massa, classe, suggestione', p. 109.

that the French sociologist Gabriel Tarde identified as a
key operator in modern social 'somnambulism', is not a
necessary vehicle of class politics—as a contemporary
populist delusion might suggest—but its nemesis. From
Benjamin, we can thus also draw and develop the idea
that revolutionary class politics consists of a technique
opposed to the fascist technologies of mass suggestion, a 'technique capable of destroying the aura of the
leader by loosening the bond of suggestion'. As Cavalletti
continues:

> Alien from the cult of the star as well as from its
> correlate, the cult of the mass, revolutionary pol-
> itics is therefore an anti-suggestive technique,
> and the battlefield and laboratory of this tech-
> nique will be once again, as logic suggests, art,
> namely, cinema and, above all, drama. [ . . . ]
> Politics, Benjamin teaches us, is a technique:
> modelled on the example of Brechtian theatre,
> it becomes capable of a revolutionary operation
> (*Leistung*), by virtue of which the mass will nei-
> ther recognize nor follow any leader [*duce*]. In
> loosening, there can be no chief, no magician or
> tempter: no psychosomatic subject can consti-
> tute itself as the centre of attraction.[27]

Class politics as the practical negation of mass psychology: this horizon remains profoundly, painfully contemporary. Benjamin once famously spoke of making
concepts 'unusable for the purposes of fascism'. Our current moment has made it urgent to carry out this opera-
tion for class too, and we can only be thankful to Andrea
Cavalletti for having devoted his scholarship and sensi-
bility to this ongoing and collective task.

---

27 'Massa, classe, suggestione', pp. 124–5.

# Bibliography

ABRABANEL, Judah (Leo Hebraeus). 'Telunah al ha-zeman' (*c.*1503) in *Mivhar ha-Shirah ha-Ivrit be-Italyah* (Jefim Hayyim Schirmann ed.). Berlin: Schocken, 1934, pp. 216–22; Italian translation: 'Lamento sopra il destino' in *Dialoghi d'amore* (Santino Caramella ed.). Bari: Laterza, 1929.

ADORNO, Gretel, and Walter Benjamin. *Correspondence, 1930–1940* (Henri Lonitz and Christopher Gödde eds; Wieland Hoban trans.). Cambridge: Polity, 2008.

ADORNO, Theodor W. 'Types and Syndromes' in Theodor W. Adorno, Else Frenkel-Brunswik, Daniel J. Levinson and R. Nevitt Sanford, *The Authoritarian Personality*. New York: Harper & Brothers, 1950, pp. 744–84.

——. 'Letters to Walter Benjamin' in Ernst Bloch, Georg Lukács, Bertolt Brecht, Walter Benjamin, Theodor W. Adorno, *Aesthetics and Politics*. London: New Left Books, 1977, pp. 110–33.

——. 'Reflections on Class Theory' in *Can One Live After Auschwitz? A Philosophical Reader* (Rolf Tiedemann trans., Rodney Livingstone et al. trans). Stanford, CA: Stanford University Press, 2003, pp. 93–110.

——. *Minima Moralia: Reflections on a Damaged Life* (E. F. N. Jephcott trans.). London: Verso, 2005.

—— and Ursula Jaerisch. 'Anmerkungen zum sozialen Konflikt heute' [Notes on Social Conflict Today] (1968) in *Soziologische Schriften* I [Sociological Writings] (Rolf Tiedemann ed.). Frankfurt: Suhrkamp, 1972, pp. 177–95.

—— and Walter Benjamin. *The Complete Correspondence, 1928–1940* (Henri Lonitz ed., Nicholas Walker trans.). Cambridge: Polity, 1999.

AGAMBEN, Giorgio. *The Coming Community* (Michael Hardt trans.). Minneapolis: University of Minnesota Press, 1993.

———. *The Time That Remains: A Commentary on the Letter to the Romans* (Patricia Daley trans.). Stanford, CA: Stanford University Press, 2005.

ANDERS, Günther. *Die Antiquiertheit des Menschen. I: Über die Seele im Zeitalter der zweiten industriellen Revolution* [The Obsolescence of Man, I: On the Soul in the Age of the Second Industrial Revolution]. Munich: Beck, 1956.

———. *Mensch ohne Welt. Schriften zur Kunst und Literatur* [Men without World: Writings on Art and Literature]. Munich: Beck, 1984.

———. *Gewalt—ja oder nein. Eine notwendige Diskussion* [Violence—Yes or No. A Necessary Discussion]. Munich: Knaur, 1987.

ARENDT, Hannah. *The Origins of Totalitarianism*. New York: Harcourt Brace, 1973[1951].

BALÁSZ, Béla. *Theory of the Film (Character and Growth of a New Art)* (Edith Bone trans.). London: Dennis Dobson, 1952[1949].

BALIBAR, Étienne. 'The Nation Form: History and Ideology' in Étienne Balibar and Immanuel Wallerstein, *Race, Nation, Class: Ambiguous Identities* (Chris Turner trans. [for Étienne Balibar]). London: Verso, 1988, pp. 86–106.

BARDET, Gaston. *Problèmes d'urbanisme* [Issues of Urbanism]. Paris: Dunod, 1948.

BATAILLE, Georges. 'The Psychological Structure of Fascism' in *Visions of Excess: Selected Writings, 1927–1939* (Allan Stoekl ed.). Minneapolis: University of Minnesota Press, 1985, pp. 137–60.

BENJAMIN, Walter. 'Critique of Violence' in *Reflections: Essays, Aphorisms, Autobiographical Writings* (Peter Demetz ed., Edmund Jephcott trans.). New York: Schocken, 1978, pp. 277–95.

———. *Gesammelte Schriften I.1* [Collected Writings, I.1] (Rolf Tiedemann and Hermann Schweppenhäuser eds). Frankfurt: Suhrkamp, 1991.

———. *Gesammelte Schriften VII.2* [Collected Writings, VII.2] (Rolf Tiedemann and Hermann Schweppenhauser eds). Frankfurt: Suhrkamp, 1991.

———. 'Schönes Entsetzen' (1929) in *Gesammelte Schriften IV.1* [Collected Writings, IV.1] (Tillman Rexroth ed.). Frankfurt: Suhrkamp, 1991, pp. 434–5.

———. 'One-Way Street' in *Selected Writings, Volume 1, 1913–1926* (Marcus Bullock and Michael W. Jennings eds). Cambridge, MA: Harvard University Press, 1996, pp. 444–88.

———. 'On the Program of the Coming Philosophy' in *Selected Writings, Volume 1, 1913–1926* (Marcus Bullock and Michael W. Jennings eds). Cambridge, MA: Harvard University Press, 1996, pp. 100–10.

———. 'Two Poems by Friedrich Hölderlin' in *Selected Writings, Volume 1, 1913–1926* (Marcus Bullock and Michael W. Jennings eds). Cambridge, MA: Harvard University Press, 1996, pp. 18–36.

———. 'The Author as Producer' in *Understanding Brecht* (Anna Bostock trans.). London: Verso, 1998, pp. 85–104.

———. 'A Family Drama in the Epic Theatre' in *Understanding Brecht* (Anna Bostock trans.). London: Verso, 1998, pp. 33–6.

———. 'What Is Epic Theatre? (First Version)' in *Understanding Brecht* (Anna Bostock trans.). London: Verso, 1998, pp. 1–14.

———. 'Commentaries on Poems by Brecht' in *Understanding Brecht* (Anna Bostock trans.). London: Verso, 1998, pp. 43–74.

———. *The Arcades Project* (Howard Eiland and Kevin McLaughlin trans). Cambridge, MA: Harvard University Press, 1999.

———. 'The Work of Art in the Age of Its Technological Reproducibility (Second Version)' in *Selected Writings, Volume 3, 1935–1938* (Howard Eiland and Michael W. Jennings eds). Cambridge, MA: Belknap Press, 2002, pp. 101–33.

——. 'On the Concept of History' in *Selected Writings, Volume 4, 1938–1940* (Howard Eiland and Michael W. Jennings eds). Cambridge, MA: Harvard University Press, 2003, pp. 389–400.

——. 'The Paris of the Second Empire in Baudelaire' in *Selected Writings, Volume 4, 1938–1940* (Howard Eiland and Michael W. Jennings eds). Cambridge, MA: Belknap Press, 2003, pp. 3–92.

——. *Walter Benjamin's Archive: Images, Texts, Signs* (Ursula Marx, Gudrun Schwarz, Michael Schwarz and Erdmut Wisizla eds; Esther Leslie trans.). London: Verso, 2007.

——. 'Che cos'è l'aura?' [What is Aura?] in *Charles Baudelaire. Un poeta lirico nell'età del capitalismo avanzato'* [Charles Baudelaire: A Lyric Poet in the Era of High Capitalism] (Giorgio Agamben, Barbara Chitussi and Clemens-Carl Härle eds). Vicenza: Neri Pozza Editore, 2012, pp. 25–6.

—— and Gershom Scholem, *The Correspondence of Walter Benjamin and Gershom Scholem, 1932–1940* (Gershom Scholem ed., Gary Smith and Andre Lefevere trans). Cambridge, MA: Harvard University Press, 1992.

BERGSON, Henri. *An Introduction to Metaphysics* (T. E. Hulme trans.). New York and London: G. P. Putnam's Sons, 1912[1903].

——. *Time and Free Will: An Essay on the Immediate Data of Consciousness* (F. L. Pogson trans.). Mineola, NY: Dover, 2001[1889].

BERNHEIM, Hippolyte. *Suggestive Therapeutics: A Treatise on the Nature and Uses of Hypnotism* (Christian A. Herter trans.). New York and London: G. P. Putnam's Sons, 1880.

BETTELHEIM, Bruno. *The Informed Heart*. London: Penguin, 1991[1960].

BIRNBAUM, Antonia. 'Between Sharing and Antagonism: The Invention of Communism in the Early Marx', *Radical Philosophy* 166 (2011): 21–8.

BLONDEL, Charles. *La conscience morbide. Essai de psychopathologie générale, 2e édition augmentée d'un appendice* [The

Troubled Conscience: Essay of General Psychopathology, 2nd Augmented Edition of an Appendix]. Paris: Félix Alcan, 1928.

———. *The Troubled Conscience and the Insane Mind* (F. G. Crookshank ed.) (London: Kegan Paul, Trench, Trübner, 1928.

BRECHT, Bertolt. 'Notes on the Opera *Rise and Fall of the City of Mahagonny*' (1936) in *Brecht on Theatre*, 3rd EDN (Marc Silberman, Steve Giles and Tom Kuhn eds) (London: Bloomsbury, 2015), pp. 61–70.

BROCH, Hermann. *Massenwahntheorie: Beiträge zu einer Psychologie der Politik* [Theory of Mass Delusion: Contributions to a Psychology of Politics] in *Kommentierte Werkausgabe, XII* [Annotated Edition, VOL. 12] (Paul Michael Lützeler ed.). Frankfurt: Suhrkamp, 1979), pp. 101–563.

BRUGEILLES, Raoul. 'L'Essence du phénomène social: la suggestion' [The Essence of Social Phenomenon: The Suggestion]. *Revue de la France et de l'Étranger* 80 (1913): 593–602.

BUÑUEL, Luis. *My Last Breath* (Abigail Israel trans.). London: Fontana, 1985.

CANETTI, Elias. *Crowds and Power* (Carol Stewart trans.). New York: Continuum, 1973[1960].

CAVALLETTI, Andrea. 'La maniera compositiva di Furio Jesi' [Furio Jesi's Manner of Composition] in Furio Jesi, *Materiali mitologici. Mito e antropologia nella cultura mitteleuropea* [Mythological Materials: Myth and Anthropology in Mitteleuropean Culture] (Andrea Cavalletti ed.), NEW EDN. Turin: Einaudi, 2001[1979], pp. 359–76.

———. *La città biopolitica. Mitologie della sicurezza* [The Biopolitical City: Mythologies of Security]. Milan: Bruno Mondadori, 2005.

———. 'Il potere della folla. Quando le masse sono pericolose' [The Power of the Crowd: When the Masses Are Dangerous], Interview with Cavalletti, *La Repubblica*, 30 July 2009.

————. 'Peut-on soigner la folie des masses?' [Can One Cure the Madness of Crowds?], *Critique* 755 (2010): 331–43.

————. *Suggestione. Potenza e limiti del fascino politico* [Suggestion: Power and Limits of Political Fascination]. Turin: Bollati Boringhieri, 2011.

————. 'Massa, classe, suggestione' [Mass, Class, Suggestion] in *Attualità di Gabriel Tarde. Sociologia, Psicologia, Filosofia* [The Contemporaneity of Gabriel Tarde: Sociology, Psychology, Philosophy] (S. Prinzi ed.). Naples: Orthotes, 2016, pp. 105–23.

————. 'Usage et anarchie' [Use and Anarchy], *Critique* 836–7 (2017): 98–114.

CHANDLER, Raymond. *The Long Good-Bye*. London: Penguin, 2010[1953].

COBB, Richard. *Police and the People: French Popular Protest, 1789–1820*. Oxford: Oxford University Press, 1970.

CONRAD, Joseph. *Chance: A Tale in Two Parts*. London: Methuen, 1914.

DARMESTETER, Arsène. 'Deux Élégies du Vatican' [Two Elegies of the Vatican]. *Romania* 3 (1874): 443–86.

————. 'L'Autodafé de Troyes (24 avril 1288)'. *Revue des Études Juives* 64 (1881): 199–233.

DEBORD, Guy. *The Society of the Spectacle* (Donald Nicholson-Smith trans.). New York: Zone Books, 1995.

DÉJACQUE, Joseph. *La Question révolutionnaire* [The Revolutionary Question]. New York: Barclay, 1854.

DELEUZE, Gilles, and Félix Guattari. *Anti-Oedipus: Capitalism and Schizophrenia* (Robert Hurley, Mark Seem and Helen R. Lane trans). Minneapolis: University of Minnesota Press, 1983.

————. *A Thousand Plateaus: Capitalism and Schizophrenia* (Brian Massumi trans.). Minneapolis: University of Minnesota Press, 1987.

DELFINI, Antonio. *Modena 1831. Città della Chartreuse* [Modena 1831: City of the Chartreuse]. Milan: Libri Schweiller, 1993[1962].

DEZNÀI, Victor. 'L'activité intellectuelle des villes' [The Intellectual Activity of Cities]. *Urbanismul* 14(11–12) (1936): 522–6.

DURKHEIM, Émile. *The Rules of Sociological Method* (Steven Lukes ed., W. D. Halls trans.). New York: The Free Press, 1982.

———. 'Internationalisme et lutte des classes' [Internationalism and Class Struggle] (1906) in *La science sociale et l'action* [Social Science and Action]. Paris: PUF, 2010, pp. 261–78.

ELIADE, Mircea. *Myths, Dreams, and Mysteries: The Encounter between Contemporary Faiths and Archaic Realities* (Philip Mairet trans.). New York: Harper & Row, 1975.

ENGELS, Friedrich. *The Condition of the Working Class in England* in Karl Marx and Friedrich Engels, *Collected Works, Volume 4: Marx and Engels, 1844–1845*. London: Lawrence & Wishart, 1975, pp. 295–583.

FALLOT, Jean. *Marx et le machinisme* [Marx and Machinery]. Paris: Éditions Cujas, 1966.

——— (Antoine Brognard). *Lutte de classe et morale marxiste* [Marxist Class Struggle and Morality]. Aubenas: Lienhart et Cie, 1968.

———. *Lotta di classe e morale marxista* [Class Struggle and Marxist Morality] (Fabio Arcangeli trans.) Verona: Bertani, 1972. Original French: Jean Fallot (Antoine Brognard). *Lutte de classe et morale marxiste*. Aubenas: Lienhart et Cie, 1968.

———. *La Science de lutte de classe* [The Science of Class Struggle] (1973, unpublished manuscript). Italian translation: *Scienza della lotta di classe* (Ivano Spano ed.). Verona: Bertani, 1974.

———. *Il piacere e la morte nella filosofia di Epicuro* [Pleasure and Death in the Philosophy of Epicurus] (Sebastiano Timpanaro introd., Anna Marietti Solmi trans.). Turin: Einaudi, 1977. Original French version: *Le Plaisir et la mort dans la philosophie d'Epicure*. Paris: Juillard, 1951.

——. *La Pensée de l'Égypte antique* [The Thinking of Ancient Egypt]. Paris: Publisud, 1992.

FLAUBERT, Gustave. *Sentimental Education* (Robert Baldick and Geoffrey Wall trans). London: Penguin, 2004.

FOUCAULT, Michel. *Mental Illness and Psychology* (Alan Sheridan trans.). Berkeley: University of California Press, 1987.

——. *Security, Territory, Population: Lectures at the Collège de France, 1977–78* (Michel Senellart ed., Graham Burchell trans.). London: Palgrave Macmillan, 2009.

FREUD, Sigmund. *Group Psychology and the Analysis of the Ego* (James Strachey trans.). London: Hogarth Press and Institute of Psycho-Analysis, 1949.

——. *Civilization and Its Discontents* in *The Complete Psychological Works of Sigmund Freud, Volume 21, 1927–1931* (James Strachey ed., in collaboration with Anna Freud, assisted by Alix Strachey and Alan Tyson). New York: Vintage, 2001, pp. 59–148.

GEIGER, Theodor. 'Panik in Mittelstand' [Panic in the Middle Classes]. *Die Arbeit. Zeitschrift für Gewerkschaftspolitik und Wirtschaftskunde* 10 (1930): 637–54.

GOYTISOLO, Juan. *Para vivir aquí* [To Live Here]. Cincinnati, OH: AIMS International Books, 1977. Original publication: Buenos Aires: Sur, 1960.

GUIZOT, François Pierre Guillaume. *General History of Civilization in Europe* (George Wells Knight ed.). New York: D. Appleton & Company, 1896[1828].

HALBWACHS, Maurice. *The Psychology of Social Class* (Claire Delavenay trans., Georges Friedmann introd.). Glencoe, IL: Free Press, 1958.

HEGEL, G. W. F. *The Encyclopaedia Logic: Part I of the Encyclopaedia of Philosophical Sciences, with the Zusätze* [1830] (T. F. Geraets, W. A. Suchting and H. S. Harris trans). Indianapolis, IN: Hackett, 1991.

HORKHEIMER, Max. *Dawn and Decline: Notes, 1926–1931 and 1950–1969* (Michael Shaw trans.). New York: Seabury Press, 1978.

JESI, Furio. *Spartakus: The Symbology of Revolt* (Andrea Cavalletti ed., Alberto Toscano trans.). London: Seagull Books, 2014.

KAFKA, Franz. 'Letter to Max Brod' (1904) in *Letters to Friends, Family, and Editors* (Richard and Clara Winston trans). New York: Schocken, 1977, p. 13.

——. 'Rede über die jiddische Sprache' (1912); English translation: 'An Introductory Talk on the Yiddish Language' in Mark M. Anderson (ed.), *Reading Kafka: Prague, Politics and the Fin de Siècle*. New York: Schocken, 1989, pp. 263–6.

LABOURIEU, Théodore [?]. *Mémoires de M. Claude, chef de la police de sûreté sous le second Empire, Tome 7* [Memoirs of Mr Claude, Chief of the Security Police under the Second Empire, Book 7]. Paris: Jules Rouff, 1882.

LAFARGUE, Paul. *Le Droit à la paresse (Réfutation du «Droit au travail» de 1848)* [The Right to Idleness (Refutation of the 'Right to Work' of 1848)]. Paris: Maspero, 1969[1883].

LAVEDAN, Pierre. *Qu'est-ce que l'Urbanisme? Introduction à l'Histoire de l'Urbanisme* [What Is Urbanism? An Introduction to the History of Urbanism]. Paris: Laurens, 1926.

LE BON, Gustave. *The Psychology of Revolution* (Bernard Miall trans.). London: T. Fisher Unwin, 1913.

LEDERER, Emil. *State of the Masses: The Threat of the Classless Society*. New York: W. W. Norton, 1940.

LEE, Gerald Stanley. *Crowds: A Moving-Picture of Democracy*. Garden City, NY: Doubleday, Page, 1913.

LEVINAS, Emmanuel. *Quelques réflexions sur la philosophie de l'hitlerisme*. Paris: Payot & Rivages, 1977. English translation: 'Reflections on the Philosophy of Hitlerism' (Seán Hand trans.). *Critical Inquiry* 17(1) (1990): 62–71.

LINDSAY, Vachel. *The Art of the Moving Picture*. New York: Macmillan, 1916[1915].

LUKÁCS, Georg. *History and Class Consciousness: Studies in Marxist Dialectics* (Rodney Livingstone trans.). Cambridge, MA: The MIT Press, 1971.

MANN, Thomas. *Doctor Faustus: The Life of the German Composer Adrian Leverkühn as Told by a Friend* (John E. Woods trans.). New York: Vintage, 1999.

MARX, Karl. *Grundrisse* (Martin Nicolaus trans.). London: Penguin, 1973.

———. 'Letter to Arnold Ruge, Kreuznach, September 1893' in *Early Writings* (Rodney Livingstone and Gregory Benton trans). Harmondsworth: Penguin, 1974, pp. 207–9.

———. *Economic and Philosophical Manuscripts of 1844* in Karl Marx and Friedrich Engels, *Collected Works, Volume 3: Karl Marx, March 1843–August 1844.* London: Lawrence & Wishart, 1975, pp. 229–348.

———. *Capital, Volume 1* (Ben Fowkes trans., Ernest Mandel introd.). London: Penguin, 1976.

———. *The Poverty of Philosophy: Answer to the 'Philosophy of Poverty' by M. Proudhon* in Karl Marx and Friedrich Engels, *Collected Works, Volume 6: Marx and Engels, 1845–1848.* London: Lawrence & Wishart, 1976, pp. 105–212.

———. 'The Eighteenth Brumaire of Louis Bonaparte' in Karl Marx and Friedrich Engels, *Collected Works, Volume 11: Marx and Engels, 1851–1853.* London: Lawrence & Wishart, 1979, pp. 99–197.

———. 'Letter to Joseph Weydemeyer' (5 March 1852) in Karl Marx and Friedrich Engels, *Collected Works, Volume 39: Letters, 1852–1855.* London: Lawrence & Wishart, 1983, pp. 60–5.

———. 'Preface to the Second Edition of the *Eighteenth Brumaire of Napoleon Bonaparte*' in Karl Marx and Friedrich Engels, *Collected Works, Volume 21: Marx and Engels, 1867–1870.* London: Lawrence & Wishart, 1986, pp. 56–8.

———. 'Economic Manuscript of 1861–63' in Karl Marx and Friedrich Engels, *Collected Works, Volume 30: Marx, 1861–1863* (Ben Fowkes and Emile Burns trans). London: Lawrence & Wishart, 1988, pp. 9–411.

———. *Capital, Volume 3* in Karl Marx and Friedrich Engels, *Collected Works, Volume 37.* London: Lawrence & Wishart, 1998, pp. 5–900.

—— and Friedrich Engels. *The Holy Family, or Critique of Critical Criticism: Against Bruno Bauer and Company* in *Collected Works, Volume 4: Marx and Engels, 1844–1845.* London: Lawrence & Wishart, 1975, pp. 5–211.

—— and Friedrich Engels. *The German Ideology* in *Collected Works, Volume 5: Marx and Engels, 1845–1847.* London: Lawrence & Wishart, 1976, pp. 19–539.

—— and Friedrich Engels. *Manifesto of the Communist Party* in *Collected Works, Volume 6: Marx and Engels, 1845–1848.* London: Lawrence & Wishart, 1976, pp. 477–519.

MILNER, Jean-Claude. *Le Salaire de l'idéal. La théorie des classes et de la culture au XXᵉ siècle* [The Salary of the Ideal: The Theory of Class and Culture in the Twentieth Century]. Paris: Éditions du Seuil, 1997.

——. *Les Penchants criminels de l'Europe démocratique* [The Criminal Inclinations of Democratic Europe]. Lagrasse: Verdier, 2003.

——. *Le Périple structural. Figures et paradigm* [The Structural Journey: Figures and Paradigm]. Larasse: Verdier, 2008[2002].

MUMFORD, Lewis. *The City in History: Its Origins, Its Transformations, and Its Prospects.* New York: Harcourt, Brace and World, 1961.

NEUMANN, Franz. *Behemoth: The Structure and Practice of National Socialism, 1933–1944.* Chicago, IL: Ivan R. Dee, 2009[1944].

PALMIERI, Giuseppe. *Riflessioni sulla pubblica felicità relativamente al Regno di Napoli* [Reflections on Public Happiness with Reference to the Kingdom of Naples]. Napoli: Raimondi, 1787.

PARK, Robert E. 'The City: Suggestions for the Investigation of Human Behavior in the Urban Environment' in Robert E. Park Ernest W. Burgess and Roderick D. McKenzie, *The City: Suggestions for the Investigation of Human Behavior in the Urban Environment.* Chicago: The University of Chicago Press, 1967[1925], pp. 1–46.

PAVESE, Cesare. 'Del mito, del simbolo e d'altro' [On Myth, Symbol and Other Matters] (1943–44) in *Feria d'Agosto* [August Break]. Turin: Einaudi, 2002[1946], pp. 139–151.

PIGUET, Marie-France. *Classe. Histoire du mot et genèse du concept des Physiocrates aux Historiens de la Restauration* [Class: History of the Word and Genesis of the Concept of Physiocrats to Historians of the Restoration]. Lyon: Presses Universitaires de Lyon, 1966.

PIROZHKOVA, A. N. *At His Side: The Last Years of Isaac Babel* (Anne Frydman and Robert L. Busch trans). South Royalton, VT: Steerforth Press, 1996.

PLESSNER, Helmut. *Macht und menschliche Natur. Ein Versuch zur Anthropologie des geschichtlichen Weltansicht* (1931) [Power and Human Nature: An Attempt at an Anthropology of the Historical Worldview] in *Gesammelte Schriften, V* [Collected Works, Volume 5] (Günter Dux, Odo Marquard, Elisabeth Ströker et al. eds). Frankfurt: Suhrkamp, 2003, pp. 135–234.

POËTE, Marcel. 'L'Évolution des villes' [The Evolution of Cities]. *La Vie urbaine* 5 (1930): 290–300.

———. 'Paris. Son évolution créatrice, I. Introduction à la vie urbaine' [Paris: Its Creative Evolution; I. Introduction to Urban Life]. *La Vie urbaine* 40 (1937): 195–220.

POUND, Ezra. 'Canto XLV' in *The Cantos of Ezra Pound*. London: Faber and Faber, 1975, p. 229.

PRAZ, Mario. *Mnemosyne: The Parallel between Literature and the Visual Arts*. Princeton, NJ: Princeton University Press, 1970.

PROUDHON, Pierre-Joseph. *Système des contradictions économiques, ou, Philosophie de la misère, Tome I* [System of Economic Contradictions, or the Philosophy of Misery, Volume 1]. Paris: Garnier 1850.

RANK, Otto. 'Ein Traum, der sich selbst deutet' [A Dream That Interprets Itself]. *Jahrbuch für psychoanalytische und psychopathologische Forschungen* 2 (1910): 465–540.

———. *The Myth of the Birth of the Hero: A Psychological Interpretation of Mythology* (F. Robbins and Smith Ely

Jelliffe trans). New York: The Journal of Nervous and Mental Disease, 1914.

ROAZEN, Paul. *Freud: Political and Social Thought.* New York: Alfred A. Knopf, 1968.

ROSSI, Pasquale. *L'animo della folla* [The Soul of the Crowd]. Roma: Colombo, 1898.

———. *Sociologia e psicologia collettiva* [Collective Sociology and Psychology]. Cosenza: Riccio, 1904.

SCHMITT, Carl. 'Die politische Theorie des Mythos' [Political Theory of Myth] (1923) in *Positionen und Begriffe im Kampf mit Weimar-Gempf-Versailles, 1923–1939* [Positions and Concepts in the Struggle with Weimar-Gempf-Versailles, 1923–1939]. Hamburg: Hanseatische Verlagsanstalt, 1940, pp. 11–19.

SCHOLEM, Gershom. 'On Lament and Lamentation' (1917–1918) (Lina Barouch and Paula Schwebel trans). *Jewish Studies Quarterly* 21(1) (2014): 4–21.

SIGHELE, Scipio. *La folla delinquente* [The Criminal Crowd] (Clara Gallini ed.). Venice: Marsilio, 1985[1891].

SIMMEL, Georg. 'Fashion'. *International Quarterly* 10 (1904): 130–55

———. 'The Metropolis and Mental Life' (1903) in *Simmel on Culture: Selected Writings* (David Frisby and Mike Featherstone eds). London: Sage, 1997, pp. 174–86.

SOREL, Georges. *Reflections on Violence* (Jeremy Jennings ed.). Cambridge: Cambridge University Press, 2004[1908].

STEIN, Edith. *An Investigation Concerning the State* (Marianne Sawicki trans.). Washington, DC: ICS Publications, 2006.

STEIN, Gertrude. 'Portraits and Repetition' in *Writings, 1932–1936.* New York: Library of America, 1998, pp. 287–312.

STEVENSON, Robert Louis. 'The Bottle Imp' in *The Complete Stories of Robert Louis Stevenson* (Barry Menikoff ed.) (New York: Modern Library, 2002), pp. 577–605.

STIELER, Georg. *Person und Masse. Untersuchungen zur Grundlegung einer Massenpsychologie* [Person and the Masses: Investigations on the Foundation of a Mass Psychology]. Leipzig: Meiner, 1929.

STOLL, Otto. *Suggestion und Hypnotismus in der Völkerpsychologie* [Suggestion and Hypnotism in Mass Psychology]. Leipizig: Veit, 1904[1894].

TARDE, Gabriel. *Psychologie économique, Tome I* [Economic Psychology, Volume 1]. Paris: Félix Alcan, 1902.

——. *The Laws of Imitation* (Elsie Clews Parsons trans.). New York: Henry Holt, 1903.

——. 'Le Public et la foule' [The Public and the Crowd] (1898) in *L'Opinion et la foule* [The Opinion and the Crowd]. Paris: PUF, 1989[1901], pp. 7–70.

——. 'Conviction and the Crowd'. *Distinktion: Journal of Social Theory* 14(2) (2013): 232–9.

VERNE, Jules. *Paris in the Twentieth Century* (Richard Howard trans.). New York: Ballantine, 1996.

VERRI, Pietro. *Sull'indole del piacere e del dolore* (1773) [On the Nature of Pleasure and Pain] in *Edizione nazionale delle opere di Pietro Verri, III, 1: Discorsi e altri scritti degli anni Settanta* [National Edition of the Works of Pietro Verri, III, 1: Speeches and Other Writings from the 1770s] (Giorgio Panizza with Silvia Contarini, Gianni Francioni and Sara Rosini eds). Rome: Edizioni di Storia e Letteratura, 2004.